To great
attitude —

Judi

Zapping the Enemy Within

Stop Stabbing Yourself in the Back

mile high
press

Also by
Dr. Judith Briles

The Confidence Factor—Cosmic Gooses Lay Golden Eggs
Zapping Conflict in the Healthcare Workplace
Woman to Woman 2000
The Briles Report on Women in Healthcare
10 Smart Money Moves for Women
Smart Money Moves for Kids
The Dollars and Sense of Divorce
GenderTraps
The Confidence Factor—How Self Esteem Can Change Your Life
When God Says NO
Money Sense
The Money $ense Guidebook
Raising Money-Wise Kids
Woman to Woman
Judith Briles' Money Book
Faith & $avvy Too!
Divorce—The Financial Guide for Women
Money Phases
The Woman's Guide to Financial Savvy
The Workplace
Self-Confidence and Peak Performance

Free articles and information on Judith's books
are available on her web site at www.Briles.com.

Zapping the Enemy Within

STOP
STABBING
YOURSELF
IN THE
BACK

DR.
JUDITH BRILES

**mile high
press**

www.MileHighPress.com

Books may be purchased for sales promotion
by contacting the publisher,
Mile High Press at PO Box 460880, Aurora CO 80046
303-627-9179 ~ 303-627-9184 Fax ~ www.MileHighPress.com

Library of Congress Catalog Card #00 136155

ISBN: 1-885331-05-3

1. Success—psychology   2. Change

First Edition

Printed in the United States of America

For Carol Ann,
my "can-do" friend

Table of Contents

Introduction

Every book has a genesis. *Stop Stabbing Yourself in the Back* was seeded as I was researching and writing *GenderTraps* several years ago. In my survey of 5,000 women and men, self-sabotage was a problem reported frequently. As I worked on the chapter about it in *GenderTraps*, it was clear this topic alone was worth discussing in a complete new book—the one that you are holding.

The Inner Snares

Several ingredients and factors enable you to sabotage yourself. These are inner snares—those old fashioned traps that lurk around the corner of life. All are situations and conditions—nooses around your neck—that you create, enforce or enable. At some time, you will encounter some or all of them, feeling that your world may be caving in. Your encounter—no matter how brief—distorts your normal, everyday range of perceptions. You end up ambushing yourself. Not a very cool thing to do.

It does not mean you are going over the deep end; that all is lost; and you are a total failure. Land mines don't always explode. Potholes don't always get bigger. Recognizing that inner snares exist and that solutions can be found means you have learned to deal with self-sabotaging issues. Some will be issues that are more likely to be female (not confronting, extreme feminists and being too personal); others more male (egomania and avoiding spirituality). Let's start by identifying the main ones.

21 Ways to Self-Sabotage Yourself

Low Self-Esteem and Self-Confidence: The lack of self-esteem and confidence paralyzes you from stretching, reaching, and seeking new competencies and challenges. Continued doses of low self-esteem and self-confidence will lead to physical and mental illness.

Momisms: Everyone grew up with *Momisms*—some innocent, some harmful. From "Eat everything on your plate because there are starving children in _____" to "Don't brag" and "Be friends," the messages you received as a kid can influence you positively and negatively as adults.

Far-out Feminists: The Women's Movement has done great things for millions of women, and contrary to what many would like to say, men have come out ahead also. But some women have taken feminism to an extreme and interpret things only one way.

Being Too Personal: Divulging too much personal information to others can lead to gossip. Others will see you as a blabbermouth who cannot maintain confidences. It can also set you up for being sabotaged by others.

Fear of Confronting: Being unwilling to confront—and even acknowledge—issues sets you up for negative self-talk, failure, even paranoia. Contrary to what many believe, conflicts are normal. What is *not* normal is how they are dealt with. The combination of learning tools and skills in dealing with conflicts expands your confidence.

Egomania: When your ego gets out of control, you have a bloated sense of your own value and importance. Couple that with immaturity and the need to get attention, and you get into trouble. Go ahead—acknowledge you have an ego, but keep it in control and balanced.

Paranoia: Being suspicious of others takes a lot of energy. It also reduces, and, in some cases, eliminates your ability to trust. This inability often holds you back from tapping into your creative talents; you just don't have the right energy for it.

Fairness: Life is not fair. Yet, every day, women and men think that what life deals them will always be fair. It's not.

Negative Self-Talk: Negative self-talk sets you up for failure. It also erodes your self-esteem and confidence. If you are in a competition of any sort, the last thing you need is to have negative thoughts running through your mind. In that competition (and it could mean just getting your voice heard at the office or a neighborhood meeting), you want to be at peak performance. Negative self-talk drains you of both your physical and mental energy.

Mind Reading: Assumptions have gotten many in trouble. Too often, you believe you know what another is thinking and feeling. Because of that belief, an inappropriate action will follow without words being exchanged.

Making Excuses: Making excuses has become an art form. Excuses are created for anything from why one is late to why "whatever." It gets to the point that when so many excuses are offered, the excuse creator actually believes them. Making excuses becomes a great way to avoid reality.

Blaming and Victimization: Seeking someone else to blame for your mistakes, inadequacies, and failures—or claiming a "woe is me" attitude—tells others you are irresponsible and immature. These are guaranteed to create a severe career rift.

Revenge: Plotting a get-even approach dilutes your energy and interferes with focusing on your work and personal life. Revenge inflames your negative thoughts, thus you live your life feeling sour and your experiences end up being negative, too. All these aspects add up to being confidence busters.

Procrastination: Putting off things—rationalizing that it's the wrong time or that you're not ready—usually means you are afraid to fail. Continued bouts of procrastination are guaranteed to block your success.

Balance: Being out of balance is a major complaint with just about everyone today. Americans work more hours in their workplaces than any other nationality. Baby Boomers introduced the concept of workaholics. We continue to say "yes" when we mean or want to say "no." The end result—we are super-exhausted.

Perfection: No one is perfect, yet far too many of us put our energies into perfectionism. Perfectionism and failure to prioritize are often companions. The end result can be chaos.

Fear of Failure: Failure is a judgment about events, either yours or someone else's. When failure occurs, the results often include the loss of self-esteem, money, and social status. Anticipating or expecting too much too soon in any endeavor can lead to failure; believing you will fail can certainly enhance its chances of occurring.

Loyalty: Gender differences surface in the job market. When a company is experiencing a change in focus or failing financially, women are more inclined to hang on until the end; men bail sooner.

Negotiation Avoidance: Avoiding using negotiation techniques can lead to personal and professional disaster. Not knowing how to negotiate—or being unwilling to enter into a negotiation—isolates you from resolving conflicts that will ultimately be in the best interests of you and your family.

Change: Change in our society increases at a faster rate as each year goes by, and it will continue to be a major factor in everyday lives. Your ability to adapt quickly to change will be instrumental in maintaining balance.

Spiritually Deprived: We all have a lot on our plate of life. Finding time for soul-searching, meditation, and/or prayer can quickly drop to the bottom of the "to do" list. By opening up to the greater universe—by realizing and accepting that we are spiritual beings—is the master in the palette of life—women and men will routinely seek guidance in their quests.

Self-sabotage impacts everyone at some time. It does not matter if you are the most successful and confident person today. There are times—hours, days, weeks, months, even years—when forces come together and create havoc in your life. By recognizing your own traps and self-sabotaging techniques, you can create the right antidote to counteract them. When you do, you will become self-reliant and self-confident—the goal of this book.

Stop Stabbing Yourself in The Back—Zapping the Enemy Within is unique in that it allows, even encourages, the reader to jump around. Each chapter is intended to "stand alone"—if you have problems with confronting—all the tools you need are in that chapter. Or, if you are looking for ways to boost your confidence, its available in a complete chapter.

In essence, you have 21 different books at your fingertips—all for the price of one!

ZAP!

Chapter One

Is There a Saboteur In You?

Sabotage is a phenomenon that permeates the air in daily living. It can undermine or even destroy your personal and professional credibility. It often results in erosion or dissolution of your self-esteem and confidence. Sabotage can be done in an overt style—blatantly for all to see—or it can take place covertly. Most often you aren't sure how it happens, much less who initiates it. You just know something doesn't feel or smell right. It's like the wind—you can feel it coming in your home, but because you don't know a storm is brewing, you demand to know who opened the window.

To understand self-sabotage, you realize what it's like to be the *target* of sabotage, whether it's delivered intentionally or unintentionally. "Intentionally" puts you at the center of a deliberate plot, while "unintentionally" results from getting in the line of fire aimed at someone else.

Possibly you aligned your loyalty, friendship or help with a prime target, unaware of the possibility that the saboteur may get you, too.

Here's another example of sabotage. Let's say you are with a group of friends and you start to talk about another person. Whether the talk is positive, neutral or negative, it's all called gossip. Except maybe for the legacy of Mother Theresa, almost everyone gossips at one time or another. What if the gossip has been distorted or embellished, or is simply untrue? If you pass along such information without verifying its truth, you have made yourself a player in the dangerous game of sabotage. Even though you did not *intend* your gossip to be damaging, the information could be dynamite in the wrong hands. And if untrue, you add insult to injury. How do you undo what you passed on?

Sabotage occurs at home. At work. Within friendships. At play. In your community. Sabotage is everywhere. So is **Self-Sabotage**. And it's your own doing. Is it possible you would undermine, erode or destroy your own credibility? Most people would say no. Yet consider these scenarios:

✓ You have made a mistake. Your common sense tells you everyone makes a mistake once in awhile. But you are having a terrible time accepting that you said or did the wrong thing. You tell yourself, both inside and out loud to others, that you are stupid, a jerk, a basic loser.

  What are you *really* saying? How about, *"I am a totally worthless human being and don't deserve forgiveness."*

✓ You have claimed a friendship with someone for years. Yet when you think of the time that you spend together, it is not very positive. In fact, your "friend" constantly berates and insults you when others are around. You, the "nice" person, just smile and say nothing.

What are your actions *really* saying? How about, *"I deserve this abuse. I'm inferior."*

✓ You have worked incredibly hard on a project. In fact, you have made plenty of sacrifices that impacted your personal life to deliver the project on time and under budget. Your co-workers and boss compliment your work. Instead of accepting their praise and thanking them, you tell them you could have done a better job if you had had more time.

What are you *really* saying? How about, *"Thanks, but no thanks . . . and no compliments. I don't deserve them."*

✓ You are on a committee that will bring a coveted entertainment event to your community for a major fundraiser. You are so excited because a close friend just happens to be a friend of the director and producer. Indeed, getting your friend to help has made everything possible. Yet when committee members offer you their "Bravos," you say, "It was nothing."

What are you *really* saying? How about, *"I don't deserve any recognition."*

Do any of these scenarios sound like someone you know? You?

Self-sabotage exists in varying degrees. On one end of the spectrum are individuals who are so destructive that nothing ever goes right for them (much less for anyone around them). Their lives are a mess; nothing makes them happy; they would rather wallow in self-pity. Remember the childhood song—

> Nobody likes me
> Everybody hates me,
> Think I'll eat some worms . . .

Written for the self-saboteur, this song becomes a mantra worn around the neck like a beloved piece of jewelry . . . never to be removed.

Midway through the spectrum are those who display self-sabotaging behavior periodically. It doesn't pop up every day, just once in a while. But when it does, it is a "doozy."

On the far end of the spectrum are others who show some form of self-sabotage, recognize it, and make a concentrated effort to avoid repeating the specific behavior.

Discovering Self-Sabotage

Are there times when you feel, or know, you are your own worst enemy? The following *Self-Sabotage Questionnaire* helps you discover where you would place your behavior on the spectrum mentioned above. Take a few minutes to read through it and answer every question. If you find some difficulty answering, ask a trusted friend to give you feedback. A word of caution: seek feedback from a caring, supportive and non-judgmental person, not just anyone.

Self-Sabotage Questionnaire

Directions:

Answer each statement according to what best describes your behavior. Score—

Never	Rarely	Sometimes	Often	All the Time
0	1	2	3	4

_____ 1. Past mistakes or failures have prevented me from accepting new tasks and responsibilities.

_____ 2. If I'm given a difficult or challenging project, I expect to fail.

_____ 3. I spend time with people who firehose down my ideas and issues.

_____ 4. I spend a lot of time talking about other people's problems, ignoring my own.

_____ 5. I get distracted easily and have difficulty focusing on what is significant.

_____ 6. At times I want to be someone else.

_____ 7. I sometimes say yes when I really want to say no.

_____ 8. I am afraid to fail.

_____ 9. When someone gives me a compliment, I often discount or refuse it.

_____ 10. When someone hurts my feelings, I want to get even with him or her.

_____ 11. I feel guilty when things are going right.

_____ 12. When I make a mistake, I find an excuse for its cause.

_____ 13. I usually expect the worst to happen.

_____ 14. When someone offers to assist me, I usually decline his or her help.

_____ 15. I often procrastinate until it's too late to meet a deadline.

_____ 16. If I don't do a perfect job, I feel I have failed.

_____ 17. If I am in a conflict with someone, I give in to keep the peace.

_____ 18. When I am negotiating with others, I let them prevail to reduce stress.

_____ 19. When something goes wrong (even if I didn't cause it), I feel responsible for fixing it.

_____ 20. When things go wrong, I blame it on others.

_____ 21. At times I realize I'm whining but I don't know how to stop.

_____ 22. When I make a mistake or something goes wrong, I tell myself how stupid I am or that I'm a jerk.

_____ 23. I believe the glass is usually half empty.

_____ 24. I am my own worst judge.

_____ 25. I believe that people who get psychological counseling are weak or losers.

_____ Add your responses for your **Total Score.**

What your **Total Score** means to you:
The lower your score, the less likely you will undermine yourself. The higher your score, the more likely you *actively* create situations that yield reversals, fiascoes and failures.

0-25: Congratulations. Your behavior shows you have a minimal inclination to undermine yourself. You are a self-confident person and can handle most land mines that get in your way.

26-50: Your behavior displays some tendencies toward self-sabotage. You may sometimes speak before you have had the opportunity to gather facts about a situation. Sometimes your mouth is in motion before your brain is in gear. To offset any self-sabotaging scenarios, have a trusted friend or a co-worker help you. Select a signal—an agreed-upon gesture or word—to alert you of an action that may lead you to hit the "self-destruct" button.

51-75: Most likely, you are a self-saboteur. Many of your thoughts and actions get in your own way. Your score shows you are a master at negative self-talk with such phrases as, "I always make mistakes; this is impossible for me to do; I knew I would blow it; someone else can do better than I can," etc. You are also a master of self-fulfilling prophecies. With negative self-talk, you can almost guarantee whatever you *perceive* the outcome to be will come to pass.

76-100: Unless you are experiencing a substantial problem or under a great deal of stress, a high score in this range spells tremendous trouble. You definitely are a self-saboteur. Your negativity and lack of belief in yourself are major obstacles to any advancement in your career, your personal life and your relationships. You need positive support, not negative criticism. Put extra effort into staying away from others who are also saboteurs and "negaholics." Pay attention to the destructive truth of this old saying: "birds of a feather flock together."

In whatever range of self-sabotage your score falls, you can focus your energy on positive affirmations and small victories. A succession of small victories can lead to increased success and major victories. And any time you have a victory . . . even arriving at a destination on time counts . . . acknowledge and applaud yourself. You have begun to eliminate self-destruction and self-sabotage.

Acknowledging you are a self-saboteur starts you on the road to recovery. Be willing to get outside help. You won't be the first person to benefit from working with a therapist who can help you remove the barriers you have erected throughout your life.

You Are More Than Just OK

If you have ever gone through a difficult time, you have probably experienced all or some of these reactions: self-doubt, paranoia, blame, low confidence, a sense of failure and a feeling that you are a victim. The phrase, "If only I had done this" or, "Why is this happening to me?" are internalized and sometimes vocalized. Everyone hears voices—those inner, self-effacing voices which are usually so subtle you barely recognize them. Yet when times are rough, it seems like someone is shouting in your ear at close range.

You will replace self-sabotaging actions with new skills that are explained in the following chapters. Let them be your new guide to personal freedom.

JB's Keeper #1
By identifying, dealing with and stopping self-sabotaging behavior, you will transition to a new you—one who routinely gives yourself permission and freedom to make mistakes and grow from them.

Chapter Two

Confidence—Who Needs It?

I often open my presentations with a story about when my underwear fell off and landed on the street after I had just emerged from a car on my way to present a morning workshop in Seattle. Audience members routinely howl as I relive my journey and its consequences. I laugh too. But I sure didn't when it happened.

In fact, I was so embarrassed and *horrified* after this incident that I would not accept any speaking engagements in the Seattle area for several years. Why? Because I thought everyone in the world had heard about my *faux pas*. My self-esteem had nose-dived.

And so had Shirley Davalos.' Not because of underwear. Because she had mentally set herself up for a fall years ago. But before you hear her story, let's look at Shirley now. Today, she is a successful entrepreneur who helps individuals put together a package profile for national publicity tours including radio and television appearances. Based in Mill Valley, California, her company, called the Shirley Davalos Broadcast Media Services is also a creator for producing segments on national TV. It enjoys a reputation of excellence.

Shirley Davalos is a star in her own right—yet she wasn't always. Years ago, she practiced the art of self-sabotage and it cost her five years on the road to achieving her professional goals.

Shirley wanted to go into television after graduating from college in the worst way, so she took her vision and hopes to the not-so-small city of San Francisco. When she interviewed with a local radio show for a job as a producer, she learned she would have to contact individuals to appear on the show. She panicked in her job interview . . . and failed to get the position. It was just one example of many setbacks that held her from her dreams. Here's how she tells her story,

> The interviewer asked me what I would do if the mayor was involved in a breaking new story. Would I call him and ask him to be on the show the next day? I told him I couldn't do that. I've never done it before. I didn't know how. Then I asked if I could start at a lower position, not as a producer just yet. He quickly replied by saying, 'Adios.' I felt crushed and discouraged, like I was a failure. It would be five years before I overcame that and got another job in the media!
>
> During those years, I worked for several banks and continued to go out on interviews. I finally landed a job as the receptionist at a local TV station. Once in the door, I went to every department and offered my services. Gradually, I was given more

work; I became a production assistant and started making the same kind of phone calls I had panicked about years earlier.

Then I learned of an opening with the local ABC television affiliate as the production secretary. It was for only a few months, replacing a woman on maternity leave. I decided to go for it. I survived, stayed on, and eventually became the production secretary on *AM San Francisco*. As the program grew in importance, so did I. A few years later, I became its producer.

If you spoke to Shirley Davalos today, she would tell you that her success comes from perseverance and being passionate about her work. Before she realized this, she had sabotaged herself. The fear of failure, the fear of criticism, the fear of negotiation, the fear of confrontation . . . even the fear of taking credit for accomplishments . . . were her constant partners. These same fears haunt millions of women today. Yet Davalos learned, as you will, that when you partner with a growing confidence in self, they can then tackle the demons of self-sabotage.

Being Your Own Worst Enemy

Self-sabotage involves doing things that do not serve your own best interests. Common phrases such as "being your own worst enemy" or "shooting yourself in the foot" are often bandied about when self-sabotage is at work. Most of us practice some form of self-sabotage at some time in our lives. Many people become quite proficient at it, knowing it's happening yet feeling helpless to stop it. The result is self-defeat and, at times, self-destruction. With self-sabotage in the picture, guaranteed, self-confidence takes a nosedive.

Confidence, or the lack of it, is the single common link in all the books I have written. Whether it is money (how to get it and how to make it grow); whether it is divorce (how to plan it and survive it); whether it is sabotage (how to identify it and remove yourself from the target range); or whether it is overcoming adversity (recognizing you can't rewind your life, you have to move on), lack of confidence is at play. That's why growing your confidence should be one of your foundations for living.

No one will knock on your door and say, "Good morning. For $19.95, I can sell you all the confidence you need. And I have an easy payment plan to purchase it." Don't we all wish it could be so easy? It's not. You have to deal with all the destructive things you do to yourself that undermine your ability to develop confidence and move forward.

What's destructive? It ranges from telling yourself you are a jerk when you make a mistake, to denying responsibility for something, to holding back from doing new activities because you fear you might fail. Shirley Davalos was afraid she would fail at the position she wanted. And I thought everyone in Seattle would know I lost my underwear. (The reality was that few people saw it happen and, let's face it, who really cares?) Both examples show self-sabotage. Building up successes over time helped them overcome the destructive results and gain the confidence needed to excel!

Shirley's experience was in the workplace but it could also apply to your involvement in a conference for your workplace or community, chairing an event or committee or a number of other activities. If you've remained in the background greeting people at the door, a new leadership assignment could be overwhelming.

Confidence, Your Palette for Life

When you become a confident and self-reliant person, you knock down the barriers that self-sabotage generates. As it fades into your past, your growing confidence becomes your palette for the future.

The words "confidence" and "self-esteem" get used interchangeably, yet there is a difference. *Self-esteem is that regard, that appreciation, that caring that you have for you.* It's your reputation with yourself. *Confidence, then, is the* **power** *to create that regard, appreciation, and caring that you have for you.* You are in charge of building and, sometimes, of demolishing, your own reputation . . . with yourself as well as with others.

Where Confidence Comes From

It's popularly believed that confidence comes from the genes you inherit and even your upbringing, especially if it's an ideal upbringing. However, the opposite is true. From a study conducted with six thousand men and women in 1989 and another 1300 plus men and women in 2001 for my book, *The Confidence Factor—Cosmic Gooses Lay Golden Eggs*, we found that confidence stems from experience—yours—birthed as a result of crises, disasters, failures . . . those tough occurrences in your life that lead to growth. In short, confidence comes from Life 101. Not a perfect upbringing. Not from genes.

In the studies mentioned above, we found a direct correlation between confidence and success—the more successful you are, the more mistakes and failures you experience, as the following example shows.

Remember back to the Winter Olympics in 1994 and the drama between U.S. figure skaters Nancy Kerrigan and Tonya Harding? During this time, no one really knew for sure if Harding played an integral part on the assault Kerrigan had suffered just seven weeks before. After taking a deliberate blow from a metal bar on her knee, Kerrigan's ability to compete in the Olympics was in question.

During an interview on national TV, she said she put all her energy into physiotherapy, training and rehabilitation for seven solid weeks before the Olympic Games. More than that, she didn't let her focus stray from her goal, despite the international attention the media showered on the assault and the rivalry with Harding.

Kerrigan stood victorious on the podium at the Olympics, taking home the silver medal, missing the gold by a small sliver. Now she stands tall as a professional skater, a wife and mom. She skates on the wings of confidence developed during this high-profile time of adversity.

How To Develop Confidence

I developed the Confidence Factor Model in my audiocassette series, *Self-Confidence and Peak Performance*. The model is shaped like five-pointed a star. The star's center is you and your issues, whatever they may be. *Self-Empowerment* is at the top, *Self-Control* at the top right, *Self-Reliance* and *Self-Improvement* at the right base of the star, and *Self-Esteem* at the left top.

Self-Sabotaging situations inhibit, encumber and catch women (and men). No place feels sacred. Since self-sabotage is self-imposed everywhere . . . at home, work, church, play, vacations . . . even driving a car can serve as a backdrop for damaging behavior and attitudes of defeat. Being paranoid, blaming others for problems you encounter, saying no to a new activity because you are afraid to fail, and practicing the art of procrastination all show self-sabotaging behavior. The antidote is confidence; it diminishes the number of times these destructive actions occur in your life.

The Confidence Factor Model

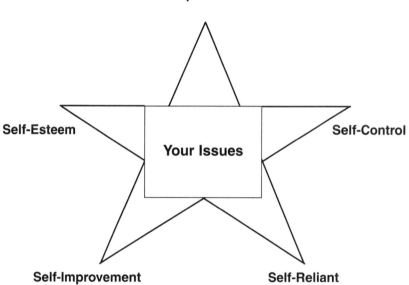

Self-Empowerment

Self-Esteem

Your Issues

Self-Control

Self-Improvement

Self-Reliant

Source: Self-Confidence and Peak Performance ©2000 Judith Briles

In the center of *The Confidence Factor Model* are your issues; at the points of the star are the behaviors described in this book . . . those that lead to self-empowerment. And when you feel empowered, you can eliminate the oppression and darkness that self-sabotaging behavior creates.

Self-Empowerment: When you feel empowered, you give yourself permission to accomplish and succeed on your own. Empowering means to authorize, enable and/or permit yourself to pursue your own personal vision. It allows you to be authentic and listen to your own voice, and not be overwhelmed by those of others.

Self-Control: With self-control, you are in charge of your destiny. If you feel you are a victim, you blame others for whatever circumstances and problems you experience. Most likely, you believe you have no control over what has happened in the past, what happens now or what will happen in the future. When you are confident, you believe you are in control of your destiny. Granted, there will be land mines and potholes along the way. But in the long run, you will be in control—the chief guide on your life-long path.

Self-Reliance: When you are self-reliant, you and others know your word is good. When you commit to a project, you do your part. You take responsibility for your actions and don't blame others if something goes wrong.

Self-Improvement: Self-improvement is ageless when you keep stretching yourself by acquiring new skills and aspiring to levels you once thought impossible. Recent studies even show that when the brain is actively learning new things, the probability of getting Alzheimer's disease lessens by 300 percent. Patience becomes an important component of self-improvement; rarely does learning a new concept or skill happen overnight. Clearly, the process can take days, weeks, sometimes months.

Self-Esteem: No matter how confident you may appear or believe yourself to be, you need to build on the reputation you have with yourself. When the potholes of life appear overwhelming, your enhanced self-esteem and self-confidence will enable you to not only survive, but pave the way to growth.

Realistically, acquiring confidence and self-empowerment takes time. As Supreme Court Justice Sandra Day O'Connor told me, her confidence came from age and maturity, from life's experiences. ABC-TV's powerhouse broadcaster Diane Sawyer told me one of her close friends daily looks in the mirror and forgives herself for the mistakes of yesterday and any mistakes she will make that day and in the future.

Eleanor Roosevelt's often quoted words, "No one makes you feel inferior without your permission," are an ideal reminder that confidence building begins with you. Use the following *Ten Steps to Building Confidence* as a daily reminder to build your confidence. You will find them loaded with common sense. And, when the chips are down, common sense is what usually works.

The 10 Steps to Building Confidence

1. *Follow Your Passion—Be True to Yourself*—Listen to your inner voice, practice positive self-talk and don't let others derail you. March to your own tune, not the tunes someone else is orchestrating.

2. *Delete Negativity*—Notice whom you work with, play with and surround yourself with. Ask yourself, "Are they energy chargers or energy suckers?" Negative people, negative things or negative work can drag you down. They can also make you sick, so eliminate them from your life. If family members are negative forces, it's critical to open communication lines with them and, possibly, engage a

therapist. NOW! Rarely do situations get better without help, but they do get worse.

3. ***Break The Rules***—Doing the "same old, same old" guarantees stagnation and career blockage. Being different sets you apart—it takes courage and confidence.

4. ***Keep on Learning***—Sign up for a class, read a book, learn to draw, enroll in school, reach out to the community and assist with its needs: the homeless, children with AIDs, domestic violence and many more. Do something outrageously different. Whatever you do, it will rejuvenate your brain cells.

5. ***You Are Never Alone***—You may feel that your pain is exclusive . . . but thousands, even millions, have walked in the same moccasins before you. People in support groups have problems similar to those you experience. Just ask to get involved.

6. ***Failure is Not Your Enemy***—What's really happened? If you lost a contract, a bid, a job, a project, received a horrible evaluation or bad news about your business, look at what's *really* going on. Is it due to a poor economy, companies merging or downsizing, and other global factors? Are you the wrong "fit" for your job? Or is it the wild card—"just bad luck?" Sometimes you can't assess the situation alone—get some feedback. Failure happens to the most successful and confident people.

7. ***Expert the Unexpected***—Shift happens—rarely does anything in "real" life play out sequentially. Step back and assess what happened, then move on.

8. ***Create Bravos***—Pat yourself on the back. Post good news in your workspace and at home. Keep a file of notes and letters containing positive remarks about your work. When crisis hits, it's hard to remember

a single good thing that has ever happened. But with your pats-on-the-back file, you have plenty of input that can encourage you. Use that praise during times when everything looks bleak. Ask yourself, "Could I recreate the same positive environment to get back on track?" Regroup, visualize the success elements of the past and determine if they fit today's circumstances. Unfortunately, many girls learned as they grew up that it wasn't ladylike to brag. Wrong input. Bragging—taking credit for the great things you do—helps build and rebuild your confidence.

9. *Keep in Circulation*—When rough times or failure hits, it is common to withdraw so the world can't see that all is not well. You may feel wounded, but don't allow yourself to be one of the "walking wounded" for long. You will heal faster if you stay involved and aim to get quickly back on target.

10. *Show Courage*—Being courageous is the key ingredient for thriving in a changing environment or relationship. With it opportunities unfold.

The Confidence Quiz

Where are you in the scheme of things when it comes of confidence—highly confident, scraping the barrel or in between? *The Confidence Quiz* below will take you only a few minutes to complete the 30 questions. Use it as an assessment to help you in understanding where you are and where you need to build yourself up.

As you read each question, write the number in the blank that best reflects how you are thinking and feeling today . . . not last week or how you speculate things may be next week. It's for *now* and will become part of your guide through the confidence maze of life.

The Confidence Quiz

Rarely or Never	Not Very Often	Occasionally	Frequently	Yes! Most or All of the Time
1	2	3	4	5

_____ Do you enjoy and thrive in the work you do?

_____ Are you your own best friend when you make a mistake?

_____ Do you acknowledge and take credit for your own accomplishments?

_____ Do you seek out and enjoy learning new things?

_____ Are you physically and mentally healthy?

_____ Are you comfortable with the way you look—with and without clothes on?

_____ Do you limit (or eliminate) your time spent with negative people?

_____ Do you surround yourself with people you admire?

_____ Do you have a trusted friend or colleague with whom you can let your hair down with?

_____ Do others routinely seek you out for advice and support?

_____ Do others enjoy being around you?

_____ Are you able to ask for something when you need or want it?

_____ Are you comfortable seeking assistance when you need it?

_____ When someone criticizes or rejects you, do you assess it, then move on?

_____ When you have failed at something, do you maintain your visibility and stay around others?

_____ When you run into problems, do you routinely handle them (or attempt to)?

_____ Can you laugh at yourself?

_____ Do you forgive yourself for mistakes that you make?

_____ Do you spend time with people who are positive on an ongoing basis?

_____ Are you able to say "no" to someone or something that you feel uncomfortable with or negative about?

_____ Are you self-reliant, asking, doing and getting things for yourself?

_____ Do you spend time on events, activities and people you enjoy and like?

_____ Do you routinely spend time to nourish your spiritual side?

_____ Do you routinely take time off for you to re-energize?

_____ Are you money smart, learning/knowing where to get advice for your present and future money needs and how to implement what to do?

_____ Do you feel that your life is in sync—balanced with work and play?

_____ Are you upbeat and positive—is life basically a joy for you?

_____ When you feel strongly (or not so strongly) about an issue or matter, can, and do you express it?

_____ Do you like who you are?

_____ Do you feel that you are "on track" for you?

Scoring:

The maximum score you can have is 150, which means you scored a 5 on everything, which is unlikely. One of the great secrets that highly confident women and men share is that there are times that they don't feel highly confident. In fact, there are times that they feel that confidence totally eludes them. Surprised? You shouldn't be.

140-150 **Extremely Confident**—You are a Confident Woman or Man. You've learned how to get, keep and grow your confidence. Bravo!

120-139 **Frequently Confident**—You have a great deal of confidence and can gain more with just a tad of fine-tuning. More than likely, you are a leader where you work and definitely have the key ingredients to move to the top.

90-119 **So-So Confident**—You're average, which yields you an average or so-so return in what you do. Why not stretch yourself and learn something new? Review your past accomplishments. It's time for you to get a few accolades, even if you are the only one applauding.

61-89 **Not So Confident**—Your confidence is shaky. It's time for you to step back and do some probing. Ask again, "Are you 'on track' for you?" and "Are you self-reliant, asking and getting things for yourself?" Most likely, you scored 1 or 2 when you initially answered these questions in the quiz above. It's probable that others control you, with your permission. You need to trust yourself and follow your passions, not others.

Below 61 **Rarely Confident**—Yikes . . . surgery is in order! You need to surround yourself with some pluses . . . at work and at home. If friends and family are dragging you down, tell them you need some positive support, not negative criticism. Treat yourself to something new. Read a great book; attend a stimulating lecture; see a fun movie. Make a conscious effort to reach out. Aspire higher!

On individual questions, if you scored less than 3 on any one, this doesn't mean that you should reject yourself. It's merely where you are today and what's impacted you in the past. Where you choose to go tomorrow is up to you. You orchestrate what steps you set in motion.

> **Self-esteem and confidence go hand-in-hand.**
> **Self-esteem is the regard, the appreciation,**
> **and the caring that you have for yourself.**
> **Confidence takes it further. Confidence is the**
> **POWER to create that respect and appreciation**
> **and regard you have for yourself.**

Throughout **Stop Stabbing Yourself in the Back**, I will reference *Keepers*, the "ahas" that I've picked from my own and others' self-sabotaging methods. Here's your second . . .

JB's Keeper #2
Where you choose to go and what directions you take are solely up to you. You, and only you, orchestrate what steps you set in motion.

Pretty powerful stuff, and yet, fairly simple in concept—let's continue . . .

Chapter Three

 Gender Differences—What Do
We Learn From Them?

Men and women differ from each other in a variety of
ways, including their psychology, behaviors and physiolo-
gy. Denying *any* differences at all gets some folks into
trouble when debating how and why men and women
differ. I say, hurrah for the differences. Can you imagine
how boring life would be if everyone were the same, with
no variables? Pretending or advocating that there are no
differences is downright absurd.

Yet making assumptions about someone based on gender often causes confusion and creates conflict. It's similar to assuming that everybody who speaks English (or
Japanese or Spanish, etc.) can be readily understood. For
instance, let's say your neighbor speaks English. Depending on his upbringing, culture, race, age, tone of voice and
use of body language, sometimes even the simplest phrases come across like he's speaking another language. And

often factors like religion or martial status influence how these phrases are interpreted. Gender is another factor that can lead to inaccurate assumptions.

Numerous books have surfaced in the last few years on gender-difference topics. Women and men hail from different planets in John Gray's **Men Are from Mars and Women Are From Venus**. In Deborah Tannen's **You Just Don't Understand,** the author explains why men don't ask directions when they get lost. The public's hunger to understand why women and men communicate differently propelled both these books onto national best-seller lists for more than a year.

Realize that each of us is unique; even identical siblings have differences. Though it may seem impossible to tell apart to the naked eye, no two thumbprints, snowflakes or DNAs are alike. Until cloning is perfected, each of us stands alone—one of a kind.

We can, though, observe some generalities. To varying degrees, we have our gender personalities, male and female. Aspects of race, ethnicity—even class—that exist in every culture compound those personalities. And behavioral traits identified as either "male" or "female" continue to influence the roles of women and men from generation to generation.

What Influences What?

Some researchers believe that gender traits reflect biochemical and biological differences that occur during prenatal development. Others believe the way the brain is organized explains the differences between men and women. And some will argue that adults pass along their gender bias to their children, serving as the primary influence on their behavior. In other words, how adolescents (and, subsequently, adults) behave reflects how society expects each gender to behave.

Do self-sabotage techniques also stem from upbringing and societal influences? Or are they physiological interactions—genes, hormones, and even the brain? The answer is "yes" to all of these. Sometimes society is the key factor; at other times the mind and body are critical. But most often, it is a combination of both. And gender differences play a role in these societal influences.

Pink and Blue Still Count

From the moment the sex of a newborn baby is known, parents, their friends and eventually society in general, respond to the child as either a "him" or a "her." Anyone who has visited a newborn in a hospital would be hard pressed to state exactly whether it was a girl or a boy without seeing the clues—pink or blue blankets and caps, or cards that say "I'm a girl, "or "I'm a boy."

Parents, relatives and friends of newborns commonly stand outside the nursery looking through the window, talking about the new family member. With society's help—that pink or blue cap, blanket or card—their comments might include: "Isn't she adorable?" "Isn't she sweet?" "Isn't she a princess?" "Isn't she precious?" "What a little doll!" "My little girl/baby." or "Isn't he a brute?" "What a winner?" "Can't you see him playing football in a few years?" "What a handsome boy!" "How's my big boy?" And so on.

Wouldn't you just love to hear this variation: "When my daughter grows up, she'll be president of this country." This sentiment is definitely an exception, not the norm. The reality is that when you think about the sweet, precious, adorable baby girl, it is hard to imagine she could grow up to be president of the United States . . . or Disney World or Microsoft. Likewise, little boys grow up under the umbrella of being both winners and bruisers

. . . and calling them sensitive or caring doesn't pop to the forefront of one's mind.

Most researchers and behaviorists in this field concur that upbringing and environment influence both the communication and behavioral styles of girls and boys. When my children were young, we lived in a courtyard surrounded by 10 houses. In one of the homes lived Sue and Jim. All the kids in our small community loved to play "Jim and Sue." They adopted Jim and Sue's mannerisms and voices—including yelling and high pitched laughing— down to a tee. All of them were incredible mimics. Their impersonations made us laugh!

From this, I learned that kids will model themselves after the dominant factors in their lives—and Jim and Sue dominated just about everyone in our neighborhood. There was nothing "mean" about the children's play. Even Jim and Sue laughed at their antics on their better days.

But the darker side of the modeling coin is abuse. It is well documented that a majority of men and women who abuse their children and spouses experienced abuse themselves as youngsters. Their environments and upbringing clearly influenced their behavior in a negative way.

Doing the Expected

For centuries, society has identified gender-appropriate roles. When women or men stepped out of those roles, it was usually temporary and often a result of an emergency situation. During World War II, for example, millions of homemakers took on the character of "Rosie the Riveter" and kept factories running while their men and sons marched off to war. When the men returned, every "Rosie" was expected to give up her job and go back to the kitchen. Most of them did.

When boys and girls (later as men and women) land in the slots deemed appropriate for them, parents and society affirm their positioning. Have you ever trained a dog? Most trainers have a pocket full of treats. When the dog responds to a specific command, the trainer offers a treat. Human beings learn in the same way, realizing that life is easier and nicer when we do what is expected.

In the same manner, we learn it's OK for girls to cry but it's not OK for boys. Because boys don't get support from others when tears surface, they learn to keep them down. Eventually, some even forget how to cry. I can clearly remember saying to my three-year-old son, who grew up in the '60s, "Big boys don't cry." That's a common phrase, even today, which is directed toward little boys. When they hear, "That's a big boy," the tears stop. This phrase serves a "treat" from mom or dad. Even today, my conditioning is so strong, I still bite my tongue if it looks like my teen grandson is on the verge of tears.

Television greatly influences most children, and the majority of programs still carry old familiar stereotypes (though some show both men and women—girls and boys—as action heroes). Children keenly observe the roles of adults in their real and TV-reflected lives. They quickly learn to mirror that behavior. This type of learning or *social modeling* becomes a significant factor in the division of gender roles.

Momisms & Dadisms Create Attitudes and Beliefs

Attitudes and beliefs about the roles of women and men were seeded in pre-historic times—when the roles of males-as-hunters and females-as-gatherers/nurturers were practiced with no questions asked. It is difficult, and some say impossible, to unravel thousands of years of imprinting.

Today, women are the primary caregivers of most young children. Even if there is a male/father in the picture for the infant, toddler or preschooler, it is still usually a female/ mom who plants the dominant seeds of future attitudes and behavior. These seeds sprout into what I call *Momisms*. Sometimes *Momisms* are right on; other times they provide the seeds of self-sabotage.

When I introduce the concept of *Momisms* and *Dadisms* to people in my workshops, participants enthusiastically dig up their own. We begin with the statement, "You should always wear clean underwear because you _____(fill in the blanks)_____ ." Of course, they always respond, ". . . never know when you will be in an accident." Or I say, "Eat all the food on your plate, because _____(fill in the blanks)_____ ." Their unison response will be "... there are starving children in Africa or China or Bosnia or Europe." (I have found the continent destination is a direct factor of how old the participant is!)

Now, how come these participants—of all ages and from multiple backgrounds—know the same responses? Do they all have the same mother? Is there a universal parenting pamphlet that recommends such responses? Can you buy that pamphlet? Would you want to buy it if you could? Not likely!

This *Momism* pamphlet of old sayings—some wise, some outdated, some downright dumb—is not one you can hold in your hand. It is unwritten, passed from generation to generation through a family's verbal legacies. Mother to daughter; mother to son; father to son; father to daughter. When you add grandparents, aunts, uncles and other relatives to the family brew, you end up with quite a stew.

Here's a partial list of *Momisms* collected over the past few years. This list is directed toward daughters:

Be nice.

Be a lady.

Be caring.

Be good.

Be sweet.

Let the boys win.

Don't fight.

Don't make waves.

Avoid conflicts.

Stay clean.

Don't wear white shoes Easter or after Labor Day.

Be careful.

Be friends.

Don't be noisy.

Don't brag.

It's OK to cry.

Cross your legs.

Be seen, not heard.

Be perfect.

Look good.

Pretty is as pretty does.

Your turn will come.

They are just jealous.

Look out for others.

Life isn't fair.

Take turns.

Don't be pushy or aggressive.

Don't compete with friends.

Good things will come to those who wait.

People will judge you by the company you keep.

It's not winning that matters; it's how you play the game.

Eat everything on your plate; children are starving in ____

Don't put a price tag on your worth.

Your face will freeze.

If you can't say it nicely, don't say it at all.

When you marry, marry for money.

Actions speak louder than words.

Two wrongs don't make a right.

What goes around, comes around.

Why get the cow when the milk is free.

Momisms (and sometimes *Dadisms*) for boys include (and are not limited to):

Don't cry.	Your "ouchie" doesn't matter.
Be a little man.	Get up and get going (after falling down).
It's OK to get dirty.	You can do anything.
Fight for your rights.	Don't be bullied.
It's OK to be messy.	It's OK to be rough.
Girls and ladies first.	Get it while you can.
Win (at any cost).	Don't throw a ball like a girl.
Don't be a sissy.	Eat your spinach and be strong like Popeye.

How about you? What *Momisms* (and *Dadisms*) were heard and practiced in your home? Think for a moment. How many can you identify? Write them down.

1. _____ .
2. _____ .
3. _____ .
4. _____ .
5. _____ .

Now, what *Momisms* or *Dadisms* have you passed on? Write down the ones you have told your kids.

1. _____ .
2. _____ .
3. _____ .
4. _____ .
5. _____ .

Much self-sabotaging behavior experienced comes from the *Momisms* and *Dadisms* of life. Some are silly—who really cares if you wear white shoes before Easter? Others—being nice, not fighting, being patient, your turn will come, be friends, share, and no bragging—all influence your attitude about yourself and your abilities. They plant the seeds of self-doubt and inhibit a willingness to confront a conflict.

What are the bottom-line results of the cultural conditioning that boys and girls go through? Primarily, women become distrustful of power and dependent on it at the same time. And men rarely show their feelings. (After all, if you had heard the message "big boys don't cry" from age two on, you may have forgotten how to cry by the time you reached adulthood. Many men have.)

As an adult, pay attention to what you say . . . to yourself and to your children. Just because you heard *Momisms* when you were a kid, doesn't mean you should pass them on to your kids without thinking carefully about them. Remember to ask yourself, "What is my specific intent when I use a *Momism* or *Dadism?*"

I believe we will always have differences in gender. And I like the fact that there are differences. As you know, there are extremes in just about everything. When we talk about genders, extremes also show up between boys and girls, men and women.

Have some fun discussing your differences. Whether you are in a relationship, married or have kids, create a discussion (lively, not hurtful) and talk about your different attitudes and habits. Where do the differences come from? Do they harm anyone (you included)? Should any attitudes or habits be changed and why? You'll be surprised with the outcome!

JB's Keeper #3
*As long as there are men and women,
there will be differences. Some grand,
some not so grand. Get over it and learn
how to work within them.*

Chapter Four

Far-Our Feminists—
How Can They Affect You?

This One's for Women!

Do women sometimes misrepresent other women's positions and views? If they do, is it intentional or unintentional? Painfully, the answer is "yes."

At some point in time, you will vocalize or endorse support for a cause. What you chose—politics, human rights, animal rights, or the environment—implies a personal interest. Supporting a cause may have an emotional as well as ideological basis, propelling a great sense of urgency to verbalize your endorsement to anyone within hearing distance.

And that is OK. But you may have experienced rejection or even outright hostility when you did so, especially if your views are not middle-of-the-road. As with any zealous communication of a controversial cause, your perceived extremism can get you in hot water.

Within this context, viewpoints on feminism abound. Life self-sabotage, the whole issue of feminism deals with empowerment, in this case empowerment of women. (Let's face it, when hasn't the subject of power *not* been a button-pusher?)

The definition of "feminism" in my Webster's New World Dictionary says: *a movement to win political, economic, and social equality for women.* I doubt many rational people who would want to deny anyone—male or female—equality. So why are the topics of feminism and feminists still such hot potatoes?

The feminist movement, also called the women's movement, heated up in the '60s. At that time, it was identified by many as the "sex-role liberation movement." Initially, it was viewed as a movement which allowed women (and men) to act in ways other than the rigid stereotypes considered "the norm" up until that time. Building broad support over time, the movement has evolved and gained greater definition.

By the '70s, various human rights movements enjoyed wide support and publicity. They brought attention and some changes to reduce discrimination based on race, culture, religion, disabilities and so on. These movements include feminist groups who were quick to take up the fight to free women from discriminatory practices.

Progress has been made and continues today. But let's consider the "extremist" position and how it affects the women's movement. If you are extremely sensitized and readily put others on the defensive at the mere hint of sexism, you may be guilty of self-sabotage. For example, a man opens the door for a woman. Instead of just saying, "Thank you," she says with reproach, "I can open my own doors." Or an office potluck lunch is in the offing. A male co-worker volunteered to coordinate the event and asks one of his female co-workers to bring dessert. Her response might be, "What's wrong? Do you think that, because I'm a woman, I bake? Men can turn on the oven too, dude."

The whole "politically correct" issue has, in my mind, been taken to the extreme. When it initially started, it seemed like a reasonable idea—that no one should be stereotyped because of gender, race, religion and so on. As a result, most people today take more care to avoid discriminatory actions and remarks. Yet now, because of the extremes, almost any form of political correctness seems a mockery. Will the progress women have made be lost? The pendulum seems to be swinging the other way because extremists have lost sight of the bigger issues.

Kissing is Not OK

Here's an example of extremism going too far in a sexual harassment case directed toward a six-year-old boy by a North Carolina school in the late nineties. His crime? Kissing a girl in his class! People around the country hooted about the absurdity of suspending Jonathan Prevette for this naughty deed. After national media appearances including a spot on NBC-TV's *Today* show, young Jonathan seem befuddled about all the hoopla . . . as well he should be. As long as I can remember, kids in the five-to-seven-year-old range have been landing pecks on the "cute" girl or boy's cheek on the school playground. To charge sexual harassment is quite extreme, especially when most kids that age don't know the meaning of sex. It's a sad commentary when little girls and boys are taught that admiring one another, flirting, hugging, and—heaven forbid—a kiss can be considered a crime.

A Few Women Don't Speak for All

Women who identify themselves as gender feminists—those who view that men, overall, are bad, and women are good—could return women to the permanent "victim" status of the past. In effect, they make enemies of men who would otherwise support the feminist cause. Some gender feminists want to subjugate men in the same way women were—but this isn't equality. If you carry this attitude, you sabotage yourself. You have clearly chosen to place yourself on an extreme side.

Since the '60s, feminist voices have written a variety of best-selling books. Betty Freidan—*The Feminine Mystique*, Gloria Steinem—*Revolution From Within*, Naomi Wolf—*The Beauty Myth* and Susan Faludi—*Backlash* comes to mind. Each has contributed enormously to the awareness of discrimination toward women. But they don't have the *only* voices.

Usually, only a few experts—voices that are often "extremist" in nature—catch the fancy of the media. Their words become the "gospel" for the particular cause they support. As a result, hundreds (even thousands) of other significant voices are never given an equal voice by the media. And that is a tremendous loss . . . for both women and men.

Unfortunately, the media loves the extremist voices . . . they make up the news that "sells." Chances are great that the majority of women are not being represented. In my opinion, the original definition of feminism—equality for women—exists in the hearts of most women *and* men. Extremism does not. So if you find yourself in a far-out position, step back and re-evaluate your opinions and posturing. You are hurting both yourself and your cause.

FOF vs. A Confident Woman

Here area few examples of positions that may hold back the Far-Out Feminist (FOF). I offer a response that is effective, less abrasive and not likely to offend:

> *Far-Out Feminist*: When someone (usually a man) says, " You look nice (beautiful) this morning," the FOF responds, "Beauty has nothing to do with value (or work). Why are you getting so personal? What do you want?"
> *A Confident Woman:* "Thank you for the compliment. What's on the agenda this morning before the marketing meeting this afternoon?"

> *Far-Out Feminist*: When a group is playing cards and one of the participants says, "This sounds like a good idea. Let's find the girls and see how they feel." The FOF jumps in and says, "Girls? Since when do we look like girls? Are you some kind of pervert?"
> *A Confident Woman:* "Gosh, I haven't thought of women as girls since I was about twelve. You are referring to all the women here, aren't you?"

> *Far-Out Feminist*: When someone asks her to bring food to a meeting (it can be asked by a man or woman), the FOF responds, "Do I look like a cook? Are you asking me to bring the food because I'm a woman? Ask Bert, he looks like he knows his way around the kitchen."
> *A Confident Woman:* "Cooking is really not my thing. If you would like some help with setting up or cleaning up, I'm your person."

> *Far-Out Feminist*: A co-worker asks the FOF out for a date. This is the fourth time he has asked, even though the FOF has turned him down before. This time the FOF responds, "I'm sick of you pestering me. If you ask me one more time, I will report you to human resources for sexual harassment."
> *A Confident Woman:* "Thanks, but no thanks. I guess I didn't make myself clear. I never mix my social life with my work life. I have made it a policy to not go out with anyone I work with."

> *Far-Out Feminist*: As the FOF gets ready to sit down, a man holds out the chair for her. She says, "Do you think I'm helpless? I'm totally able to take care of my own needs."
> *A Confident Woman:* "Thank you."

As you read through the above scenarios, can you recall when you have observed behavior similar to that of the *Far-Out Feminist*? Have you responded in ways that the *Far-Out Feminist* might? Do you think the responses from *A Confident Woman* can be as effective as the more abrasive style of the *Far-Out Feminist*? Why or why not?

When It's Critical. . .

If you find yourself taking a FOF position that you truly believe is important, even life threatening, you may argue, "This is critical to me, as a woman." You have a right to your view. What then, is the next step in presenting your position or opinion effectively? Here are a few questions to consider first:

✓ Have you identified who has the power to change the situation you are concerned about?

✓ Do you have the time and energy to focus on the process that will bring your cause to a solution or completion?

✓ Have you identified other sources that support your position?

✓ What kind of connections and power, if any, do they have?

✓ Do you know the history and background of the change you want to make? Why is it the way it is?

✓ Has anyone else complained or attempted to change the situation? How did they do?

✓ Do you know what others have done in the past in their attempts to change the situation?

✓ If there is a denial of what you are seeking, what will your next step be?

✓ Finally, is this the most important battle you can/want to put your energies into?

It is essential for you to know that you do not have to sacrifice your ideals or values. If you recognize a problem that could escalate, heed the warning signs. You can respond to others in a way that educates them. Try a little humor; it may sweeten your point of view and help the medicine go down. Apply the questions above to your situation and get help if you have found a worthy cause to champion.

Many women don't view themselves as feminists, yet they are. Women today assume their objective is equality in pay and opportunity, a primary goal of feminism. And many women today feel alienated by the radical voices that are routinely highlighted in the media. I find myself in this sector. Women that I work and play with are more likely to view themselves as humanists . . . demanding equity and opportunity for all without verbally or physically bashing others, including men.

The bottom line is to weigh your words and your actions. Their impact on others may act counterproductive as to what you really want to say.

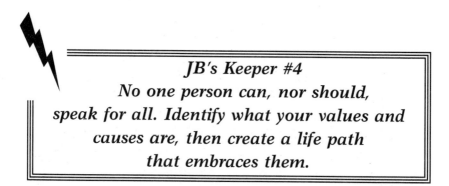

JB's Keeper #4
No one person can, nor should,
speak for all. Identify what your values and
causes are, then create a life path
that embraces them.

Chapter Five

 Betrayal—Everyone Is
Not Your Friend

If I were asked to identify a single trait that more women have than men—the one that can leave them walking on eggshells—misinterpreting friendship ranks at the top of the list. "Surely, you must be kidding?" is your probable initial response. But, I'm not. Hear me out.

Since the mid-'80s, I have conducted six national studies on workplace issues. Each one tapped into women's friendships with other women. The results from those studies appeared in *Woman to Woman 2000—Becoming Sabotage Savvy in the New Millennium, Woman to Woman: From Sabotage to Support, The Briles' Report of Women in Healthcare, GenderTraps* and *The Confidence Factor.* There is absolutely no question that women have wonderful friendships with other women. And, there is also no question that women have had very painful experiences in associations they thought were friendships with other women.

For years, men have been criticized about their friendships . . . or lack of them. Truth be told, men have friendships, some quite deep. The difference between male and
female friendships is multiple. Men are less likely to reveal personal and intimate information as freely as women
do. Because men are less likely to reveal personal information to just anyone, they are less likely to feel betrayed
by another. In the final episode of *Survivor* during the
summer of 2000, the final two women took their loss of
the $1,000,000 far more personally than the men did,
"How could you betray me and vote for him?" As the men
were knocked off the island, they didn't talk of betrayal.

My research has found that women confuse friendships with acquaintances, I have found they tend to talk
too much, too soon. They often reveal very intimate details of their lives to someone (at times, anyone) before
they really know that person. After all, Mom said to be
friends, to be nice, to share.

As a rule, men don't get caught in the "revealing it all"
trap as women do. They are far more inclined to view
their many acquaintances as merely acquaintances where
women often view them as friendships. Men usually
don't confuse friendship with friendliness.

Too many women assume that, because they are women,
friendship (which implies trust) is a given. Women often
"chat" and find they have a commonality of experience and/
or philosophy and then, in a nano-second, feel they have
forged lifetime friendships. That's the exception, not the
norm. The great majority of friendships take time to evolve
and develop. A true friend is a rare treasure.

Because women tend to divulge *far* too much personal
information to relative strangers, they often experience a
deep sense of betrayal when intimate and confidential details become public knowledge. Why? Because they trusted

an acquaintance who wasn't a friend. The situation between Linda Tripp and Monica Lewinsky which fueled a scandal in President Clinton's White House in early 1998 reveals a modern-day example of trust betrayed. Not only did Tripp listen to Lewinsky tell her confidential story on the phone as a "friend;" she tape recorded the conversation and made it public.

A friend doesn't reveal personal or secret information. If you have been betrayed, simply know that that betrayer was never a true friend. The solution is to be discerning with your trust. Take your time when developing relationships . . . time to determine the fit you have with another's values, concerns, hopes, fears, and even dreams.

Ask: What is your link? Do you have shared values? What about common interests? After you have satisfying answers to these questions, make sure you delve deeper. Does she frequently realign her friendships or relationships with other women—this week she is Marge's friend, next week Briana's and the following, Fred's? Does she talk about others, often revealing information you think is a tad too personal? Does she make you uncomfortable by asking questions that you feel probe too deeply? If you answered "yes" to any of the above, this chapter is for you.

What kind of friend are you? Do you ever ask acquaintances questions that could be construed as very personal? Do you ever gossip about others—revealing information that is probably confidential? Have you, or do you, realign friendships? Do you ever feel (or has someone you trust told you) that you talk too much? If you have any "yes" answers, definitely read on.

In many ways, this chapter is painful for me to write because it reveals the dark side of women. You will read about women who were political and held prominent positions; women who communicated regularly; women who shared intimate secrets and concerns; women who *assumed* friendships because of their common gender. Although more than four hundred years separate the two stories which follow, the four women involved could have switched centuries.

Both Queens, One Survives

In 1933, Maxwell Anderson wrote *Mary of Scotland*. In this play, the Catholic Mary Stuart has decided to return home from France after the death of her husband, the King of France, to rule Scotland. Her cousin, Elizabeth, a Protestant, is the Queen of England. She is determined that Mary will not be Scotland's Queen. The Earl of Bothwell, Mary's friend and supporter, urges war against the Protestants as the only way to insure control for Mary. Mary, who is both idealistic and naive, insists that, "She (Mary) will win, but . . . in a woman's way, not by the sword."

At the same time, Elizabeth has concluded that any outright war against Mary would not be desirable. Instead, Elizabeth uses cunning and ruthlessness as weapons to remove Mary from her throne and eventually bring about her death. Elizabeth first turns Mary's supporters against her. Still Mary, who has vowed to "rule gently," trusts her cousin, the Queen of England, too much. As a sign, she treasures a ring sent by the queen as a pledge of friendship. She doesn't believe betrayal is possible even when told of it, and eventually falls into Elizabeth's snare.

In the end, Mary can no longer deny Elizabeth's duplicity, but continues to insist, "Thrones fall that are built with blood and craft," and, "What I am, will be known. What's false will wash out in the rain." In Anderson's version of the confrontation between the two queens, Mary queries her cousin, "But does this mean you can lend no hand to me?" And Elizabeth responds,

> One's a young girl, young and harrowed as you are—
> one who could weep to see you here—and one's a
> bitterness at what I've lost and I can never have, and
> one's the basilisk you saw. This last stands guard,
> and I obey it. Lady, you came to Scotland a fixed and
> subtle enemy, more dangerous to me than you've
> ever known. This could not be borne, and I set
> myself to call you out and down, and down you are.

Mary warns Elizabeth she will not be able to continue with the masquerade, that nations will find out what she's done, men will know, even God. Elizabeth counters her threat,

> Child, child, it's not what happens that matters, no,
> no, not even if what happens is true, but what men
> *believed* to have happened. They will believe the
> worst of you, the best of me . . . all history is forged!

Mary's response, as she goes to her room before being taken to meet her death, speaks clearly to many women today,

> This crooked track you've drawn me on, cover it, and
> let it not be believed that a woman was a fiend.

When Mary first knew of Elizabeth's betrayal, she was sure Elizabeth would come to her senses and offer support—after all, they were cousins . . . women . . . sisters. But later, Mary's only comfort was to believe that what goes around, comes around, that truth will prevail in the end. She was the victim of *Momisms*. "Be friends, share, be patient—your turn will come, don't fight, and avoid conflicts." And each of these *Momisms* is alive and well centuries later.

We have women so very like Elizabeth and Mary in our lives today—Elizabeths spreading scandal and dealing in half truths; Marys, naive and incredulous victims of their more envious "sisters." Even though there are perpetrators and victims, both types of women are at risk because both become victims of the rivalry between them.

Today's Marys suffer frustration, anger and resentment. All too often, they have a need for a revenge that is self-defeating and speeds up the victories for the Elizabeths in their lives. And what of these Elizabeths? Often their successes are not as sweet as they might have hoped. Sometimes the sabotage that won them early victories blinds them, thus deterring their progress to their true goals.

The Gossip Connection

Many women initiate friendships through gossip. Elizabeth and Mary were both masters at generating gossip about each other. It requires no special skills or tools—just a mouth or email system.

Just how prevalent is gossip? *Self* magazine surveyed its readers and found that 74 percent stated they liked to gossip. When asked what they usually talk about, 61 percent said goings-on at work, 44 percent said their friends' personal lives, and 40 percent said people they disliked.

Their overall thoughts about gossip? Sixty-four percent of the respondents said it was a harmless diversion and usually a lot of fun. Only 24 percent felt it was destructive and malicious while 22 percent said gossip was petty or a waste of time. Fourteen percent of the respondents felt it was a practical way to get the office scuttlebutt. (Note: Totals exceed 100 percent due to multiple answers.)

The old adage, "Sticks and stones can break your bones, but names can never hurt you," is a myth. Words *do* hurt when passed on irresponsibly. Attempts to disprove the validity of gossip rarely reverses the damage already done. Loose tongues ruin reputations, family relationships, friendships, and even careers.

Now, do men gossip? Of course they do. But the primary difference between men and women is that men don't care about the personal details. They are more likely to view gossip as information—the grapevine. Does it—the gossip—affect work or self personally? If it doesn't, then it's a pass—not to be bothered with. Are there men who really like to dish—passing any and all info along? You bet, but they are in the minority.

Are Women Really Barracudas?

Politics will always be with us. In 1998, the media went into a frenzy over the shenanigans between President Clinton and former White House intern Monica Lewinsky. Over several months, Tripp taped her phone calls with Lewinsky—more than 20 hours worth. She even met Monica for lunch wearing a tape recorder and set Lewinsky up with federal agents to use the taped conversation.

When was the last time a close friend of yours taped your calls without your knowledge or permission? When was the last time a friend invited you for lunch, intending to tape you and set you up to the FBI? I suspect never. But that's exactly what Linda Tripp did to her good friend Monica Lewinsky, who never suspected a thing nor imagined herself in hot water in the eyes of the nation.

I have interviewed thousands of women who have been undermined by other women under the guise of friendship. A few stand out. One was Rita Lavelle. I first met her in 1986 when she was serving time in a women's prison in Northern California. Her crime? She had "lied" to Congress four times. She was accused of telling the same lie to four committees. Congress charged her with perjury, and off to the slammer she went.

Now, with all the nonsense and baloney Congress feeds to the American public, I find it ludicrous that its members can charge anyone with perjury. But indeed they did. The saga of Rita Lavelle displays deception, manipulation and almost a blind faith about supporting another woman just because she is a woman.

Her story begins on a high . . . in her key and visible position in the United States Environmental Protection Agency (EPA). Her division regulated environmental aspects of business. She noticed early in her employment that her boss, Anne Burford, the agency head, had a number of problems. Within six months of accepting the post, Burford had fired four of the administrators she had hired. Burford made it her primary job to be highly visible in the Washington political scene. But when it came to doing her job as agency head, she just wasn't performing—at least not well.

Burford was constantly at loggerheads with her administrators over some issues or another. Lavelle said,

> I realize now—I didn't at the time—that our motivations were in direct conflict from the beginning. While I was seeking to prove I could be a successful manager—harnessing and directing the technical talent of the agency, freeing it from the bureaucratic red tape so elaborately woven by the attorneys—Anne sought to become the hottest female political figure in the land.

In an agency like the U.S. Environmental Protection Agency, whose actions (or lack of action) so dramatically affect the quality of life for all citizens, this conflict spelled disaster. All my activities were designed to provide the meat; all of hers, to attract the sizzle.

According to Lavelle, not only did Burford have trouble with follow-through on the job, she was rarely in the office when she should have been. She continues,

> Anne had no interest in follow-through on projects and was often unavailable to her managers for weeks on end. Failing to realize she felt follow-through was completely unimportant, I mistakenly made excuses for her when she really sought none.
>
> We almost became the antithesis of each other. I was working 16 hours a day to get results. She appeared at the office less and less, but when she did, it was always in a dramatic fashion. I was soft-spoken, conservative and always promoting others as a means of achieving results. When necessary, I could come down hard and say no, demand accountability or improved self-discipline. But I was never at ease in center stage.
>
> When I worked out an excellent agreement with an assailed Democratic governor that not only protected the environment and local jobs but also his political career, she attacked me as disloyal to the White House. 'How dare you let him announce that decision,' she screamed. 'He is a vulnerable incumbent. We could have used the firing of all those people to crucify him at the polls. You had better learn the game or get out.'

According to Lavelle, Burford was used to hearing compliments from her personal staff members. She wanted her administrators to compliment her, too. When they didn't, she became annoyed, as Lavelle explained,

> Rather than seeking management input on direction and policy, Anne sought constant feedback on how she personally was perceived. She forbade meetings between more than two of her administrators without her presence. Rather than convening meetings herself to resolve policy disputes or provide direction, she relied on her staff to bring news of her administrators' performance, especially since she was out of the office so often.

To some extent, Lavelle felt Burford's behavior was due to her being under a great deal of personal pressure, including an ugly divorce. Burford became physically ill, taking many weeks off work to recuperate. Out of loyalty and concern, Lavelle tried to help Burford both personally and professionally, like assisting in getting the court records sealed during Burford's custody fight.

Lavelle believes that Burford became increasingly envious and hostile toward her because she was performing so well at a time when Burford was not. Burford's haphazard management style contributed to the problem. In Lavelle's words,

> Anne felt very vulnerable and rather insecure in her position. While she is a very gifted woman—very talented, articulate and physically beautiful—she got there totally on her politics. She really didn't even know that much about the work of the agency, didn't

care to become involved and, frankly, wasn't even part of the decisions made day in and day out.

Under these circumstances, the agency was wrecked by Burford's 'me-against-them' policy. When political pressures mounted against her, Lavelle concludes Burford found a scapegoat: her. In Lavelle's view, Burford settled on her out of jealousy and envy because Lavelle was doing well managing the most successful program in the whole agency. Burford's prestige and authority were eclipsed by Lavelle's good results.

I had my job to do. She reviewed my budget, she reviewed my performance standards, so it was ludicrous to claim I was performing in a manner she had no knowledge of or could disagree with.

In retrospect, Anne's criticisms of me were always related to externals—my dress, my makeup, and my speech mannerisms. I never realized why it hurt so much, but now I can see that while she would attack me for areas in which I felt so sensitive, she would never acknowledge the strengths I considered so important—my program results. Thus, her criticism and absence of praise combined was devastating.

I remember one exchange in particular. After she had a heated four-hour session before an abusive Congressional chairman noted for his rudeness in conducting hearings, Anne cooed, 'I never have a problem with him (the chairman); I just get dressed up and bat my eyelashes, asking for help and sanity from his committee. He especially likes purple and it photographs well.'

Lavelle believes that as soon as bad publicity hit about the agency in general—sparked by political infighting in Washington—Burford used her to take the heat off herself. Lavelle's success had made her feel more vulnerable and insecure within herself.

> Some of us administrators had talked about the fact that Anne would probably seek a scapegoat and each of us thought it was going to be one of us at a given time. However, everybody was shocked that the scapegoat would be me, mostly because my program was so successful and she was claiming credit for it all over the country. So I had assumed I was safe. There was total shock when it came down on me.
>
> Anne told the Justice Department that 'Rita held up the grant and embarrassed the Administration,' and that she couldn't continue with Rita in her present position.
>
> Having worked overtime to deliver results, I was now devastated by the personal attacks delivered on the front pages daily by 'anonymous' sources. Nevertheless, I was still an ingrained team player. As Anne attacked, I continued to defend her and my now-silent teammates—right up to the time I was indicted for 'lying to Congress' about the date of a meeting.
>
> I asked why I should have lied about a completely innocuous date, still studiously refusing to criticize Anne whose actions *had* been significant in the case in question. Sinking further into shock and disbelief, I was unable to convince a jury that I didn't lie. The chief prosecutor claimed—with no evidence—that I had engineered the date discrepancy in return for a 'big bucks job' after I left government. I was

sentenced to six months in prison, five year's probation and community service, a $10,000 fine, attorneys' fees that I will never be able to pay, and a lifetime label of convicted felon.

Indeed, once Burford began to attack Lavelle, she continued by embarrassing her with her peers and pillorying her in public. Before the political uproar, Lavelle had told Burford she wanted to go into private enterprise after her appointment was up, in particular become vice-president of a particular company. Burford used this confidence to hang her.

> Now, why did she do this to me? Because she felt threatened for her own job and she thought I might be named the replacement. In plain English, I had done everything politically that she was supposed to have done, and we were in a very successful position.

What particularly galled Lavelle was her persistent loyalty to Burford. She had done everything in her power to cover up for her when Burford was lax. She had done this because Burford was a woman and an assumed friend. Lavelle strongly felt that 'sisters' should support one another.

> I would say that I was like a sister to her; that's how I felt. That is why the whole thing flabbergasted me.

Lavelle, along with many of those we interviewed, feel that women are less likely to separate personalities and issues. When the chips are down, women more likely personalize what happens, intensifying the retaliation of those who opposed them. Burford, under a great deal of pressure, already felt insecure, vulnerable and scared. Lavelle, a successful woman who threatened to overshadow Burford, was singled out for the brunt of her boss' attack. Her previous loyalty and performance counted for nothing.

Lavelle ended up doing a term in jail for lying to Congress; Burford managed to get off practically scot-free. She accused Lavelle of various crimes after she pled guilty to some charges. Burford was given immunity when she agreed to say she was guilty of some things, so the government never prosecuted her. To the public, she appeared the victim, not Lavelle.

Can you relate to Rita Lavelle's story? Granted, not everyone goes to jail when set up by a "friend." There are, though, shared experiences. Lavelle felt a huge sense of personal betrayal. She had helped Burford out, covered for her. She kept asking, "How could she do this to me?"

In reality, Burford wasn't Rita Lavelle's friend ever. She was a competitor and afraid that she was in trouble. Lavelle became the scapegoat. She was in the wrong place at the wrong time.

Oprah, Ross and the Security Guard

When I appeared on *Oprah* to talk about women and sabotage in the workplace, Rita Lavelle was one of the guests. While she was telling her story, I waited behind the curtain prior to my introduction as the "expert" on the topic. As we both viewed the monitor, the security guard said, "You women just don't get it." When I asked him what "get it" meant, his response was, "When we men set somebody up, we take care of them when they get out."

I never forgot his words. In 1992, when Ross Perot was on *Donahue* during the presidential campaign, Phil

Donahue asked what Perot had told Oliver North during the Iran-Contra hearings. Perot responded, "I told Ollie to tell the truth. If he went to jail, I would take care of his family, and when he got out, I would guarantee him a job."

Now how did that security guard from Chicago, Illinois, know what Ross Perot from Dallas, Texas knew? They both are men and they know that if there is a scapegoat or a fall person, one of the rules—unwritten—is that you "take care of them when they come out." Why don't women know this rule? Men seem to.

Over a decade has passed since Rita Lavelle first set her foot inside a prison. She is still trying to put her life together, this time with the word "felon" attached to her name. Lavelle's lie to Congress concerned a date. She couldn't pinpoint the exact dates of some meetings because her calendar had mysteriously disappeared. Was there a calendar? Indeed. It showed up in the back of Attorney General Ed Meese's safe when he left the Reagan Administration. Too late. And, who stole it?

Today, Rita Lavelle is the founder and CEO of Nutech, a California-based company that specializes in getting rid of toxic waste in private industry. In a recent conversation, she told me she is often in strategy meetings that include other groups competing for the business. Even now, derogatory comments or innuendoes about her past come up—most usually when women competitors are part of such meetings. The quality of her work now carries an excellent reputation and speaks for itself. There are never questions, innuendoes or inferences from men, *only from other women.*

On *Oprah*, Lavelle said, "The whole experience was equivalent to an out-of-body nightmare." When Oprah asked her why she covered up for her boss Anne Burford, she responded, "It was to help a sister. Then, there were very few of us back there (Washington, DC)." Lavelle also said if she had been warned she would be the sacrificial lamb, she would have tolerated the situation better than she did. Rita Lavelle's dream is to clear her name and become a non-felon. Only time will tell whether she ever gets her pardon. I was hoping President Bill Clinton would end her painful saga when he granted the traditional pardons as a President leaves office. No such luck. Maybe the next Administration.

Being Friendship Savvy in the Workplace

The Friendship-Friendliness Quiz identifies ten questions you should ask yourself. These questions relate to relationships with others in and out of the workplace, women and men you may develop friendships with.

The Friendship-Friendliness Quiz

1. Do you ever reveal personal information to someone that you have just met?
2. Would you feel betrayed if a potential new friend told someone else a personal story or revealed anything you considered intimate?
3. Would you feel excluded if that new friend went to lunch with another friend or co-worker and didn't invite you?
4. Would you feel overlooked if he or she forgot your birthday?
5. Would you cover for him if you knew he was having personal problems?
6. Would you allow her extra time to complete projects you had asked her to do, if you were her supervisor or chair of a committee project?

7. Would you feel uneasy if you needed to criticize her?
8. Would you feel bad or angry if he criticized you?
9. Would you feel left out if he dropped out of your committee, transferred to another department or moved to another city?
10. Would you feel uncomfortable competing for a position against her?

A *yes* answer to any of them indicates that your personal expectations of others carry a "strings-attached" awareness when building your friendships. But a *yes* answer *does not* mean that you shouldn't develop friendships with others in your workplace. Instead, it means you should look for some hooks within the potential friendship—those "attached strings." One *yes* or more means you may have to be more sensitive to your relationship; hurt feelings could spill over and a domino effect could (and most likely would) impact you both.

JB's Keeper #5
Recognize that friendships are a luxury.
It is also imperative to understand that
not everyone is "friend" material.

There is a difference between friendship and friendliness. Be cordial and gracious to others. Don't, though, reveal your concerns, fears, hopes or dreams to all. Be discerning with those you choose to trust. And truly value those you do.

Betrayal is always a difficult topic—especially when there are few clues that lead up to it. If being betrayed, undermined or sabatoged by another is a concern or issue for you, I strongly encourage you to get my book *Woman to Woman 2000—Solving Sabotage and Betrayal in the New Millennium.*

The entire book is dedicated to the who, what, where, when, and why of sabatoge . . . and methods to realistically deal with it.

Note

1. Maxwell Anderson, *Mary of Scotland*, New York: Anderson House, 1933, copyright renewed in 1960 by Gilda Anderson. All subsequent references are to this text and are used with permission of Gilda Anderson.

Chapter Six

Confrontation—You're Just Too Nice to Make Waves

Confronting another person is rarely high on anyone's priority list. When most women get involved in a negative situation, they seldom "have it out" with the person who created it. Instead, they tend to grumble about it to a friend, a colleague or a spouse. Men tend to do one of two things. Either confront the issue, or they let it roll off their backs.

Little girls are taught not to fight, complain or make waves. *Momisms*—the big lessons of early childhood—have carried over into womanhood. But the belief that nice girls do not use confrontation is a myth. The reality is that everyone *can, should* and *do*.

Another myth is that if people care for each other—whether at work or within friendships, relationships and families—there won't be conflicts. Instead, harmony reigns . . . at all times. If you believe that, I have some swamp property I'd like to sell you.

What happens when you don't confront each other in a healthy manner? Several examples follow.

Tomorrow Is Another Day

Tom is a RN working in a female dominated workplace. He finds the team in the operating room where he works is a fairly clannish group. When there's a problem, work-related or personal, he sees that few women want to deal directly with it. They are more likely to ignore it until it festers and becomes a pain in everyone's side. The Scarlet O'Hara approach is their motto, "Tomorrow is another day." Tom's words,

> Let's say I have done something that makes someone angry. Instead of that person coming to me and saying, 'I'm angry at you because you didn't do this right,' she will talk to someone else about me instead.
>
> Before I know it, the whole unit is buzzing. The information becomes second hand, third hand, fourth hand and so on. It builds up. When it finally comes back to me, it's so blown out of proportion; I barely recognize the original incident.
>
> I've told the women I work with I expect to hear about a problem now, not six months later. My male colleagues don't play games.

Unjustified Accusations

Today, Sally is mom to four kids under the age of 12. Before she had them, she was a teacher. She remembers when she was completing her teaching credentials. One of the other women in the class accused her of trying to seduce one of the professors to get a better grade. In Sally's words,

Now, this woman didn't launch an accusation when we were alone. She did it in front of a room of classmates . . . the day before my final exam. It was a bad scene.

Accusations are difficult to deal with—and nearly impossible to respond to—when they come at you publicly and without warning. If this happened to you, you would be paralyzed—momentarily stunned. And if you don't respond in anger, public opinion convicts you whether you're guilty or not.

Women, because of their non-confrontational style, usually don't think quickly in a situation like this. But let's look at what could be done. In Sally's case, a playful comeback could be, "I wish I'd thought of that. He's a hunk." She could admit she was caught off guard, then diffuse the accusation with some humor.

Lack of response or an angry comment can create really bad scenes. Even worse is letting your anger set in and putting your mouth in gear before your brain has a chance to catch up with your feelings.

Sally wasn't able to confront her accuser. Her lack of action in this case—and probably in other confrontational situations—fostered feelings of depression that solidified into her belief system of self-deprecation. As she shared,

I felt like I was a rotten human being. I did not have the strength at that time to confront her. Instead, I severed all relations with her. This was many years ago. Within the last couple of years she tried to contact me, and I made it very clear I did not want anything to do with her.

Anger held onto for a long time does nothing for your self-esteem. Sally could have vented a little then offered the forgiveness her attacker from the past was most likely seeking. Sally "cut off her nose to spite her face." If you were sabotaged when your self-esteem wasn't at the level it is today, you could miss out on the opportunity to purge the old hurt and anger.

And what if your accuser really *had* changed. You might miss out on something good. Saboteurs are usually subject to immaturity and insecurity. They can change. So can victims . . . avoiding years of hard feelings and, at times, ugly and revengeful thoughts.

Creating Rumors

Robert felt he had a good working relationship with the other committee members (mostly women) to raise funds for the high school band trip to the Rose Bowl for the annual New Year's Day Parade. Others on the committee told him one woman was actually fabricating stories about him. Stories focused on both his present management activities and past interactions where the two had worked on another community event. Robert knew these rumors were untrue. As he explained,

> I don't know if there was envy or jealousy, or
> if she just didn't like what I did as a supervisor.
> Eventually I was able to go to her and discuss the
> rumors.
>
> I told her if she had concerns on how I
> handled a specific situation that arose— she needed
> to come to me first, not to others. I told her I
> wouldn't say anything to anyone else; that I would
> respond directly to her face. I expected the same
> from her.

Women who undermine other women don't want them to be successful. Jan was one of 25 candidates for a position and she did not know who the others were. But she was able to identify them after she was promoted. As she told the story,

> I found out fast who also applied after I got the job. When several women acted rudely and tried to block things, I learned they had been finalists. But what was hard to comprehend is why my former boss was telling people I was a 'spy' and a 'snake.' We had always gotten along and she had given me high ratings on my evaluations.

When anyone gets caught with their hands (or mouth) in the cookie jar, it's uncommon for them to stand up and declare they did it . . . whatever "it" is. Jan continued,

> After I went to a conference on communications for women in the workplace, I decided to get a discussion going with my former boss about her behavior. She was surprised by the depth of information I knew about her activities, told me by my secretary. She had looked at the rules differently for herself than for others.

JB's Keeper #6
Conflict is normal . . . what sets
a person or organization apart is
in the way it's acknowledged and managed.

Characteristics of Conflict

Conflict between people has several traits and characteristics. As a conflict escalates, concern for "self" increases in a parallel manner. Then the "desire to win" increases with this rise in self-interest. If conflict escalates, "saving face" commonly takes on more importance.

When dealing with someone you are going to confront, personally or professionally, first identify the strengths and weaknesses by understanding the preferred style for handling conflict by the other party. It means you have to step back, change hats and put yourself in his or her place by anticipating responses and reactions.

Techniques for handling conflict vary. What works at a low level of conflict can be ineffective, even counterproductive, at a high level of conflict. Even within a conflict, people can draw on different styles for handling it.

This chapter is big. Because it's critical to learn to confront another more effectively, I've chosen to present material that I use in a normal multi-hour conflict and solutions training session. If you don't confront issues your silence grants approval.

It would be helpful to become aware of your own conflict style. Below is the *Managing Conflict Styles Questionnaire* that I often use in training workshops that focus on creating collaboration out of conflict. Your score will determine what your conflict style is. The style that has the greatest total indicates your dominant style in dealing with conflict; the second highest total will be your backup, secondary style. Take time to go through this questionnaire now.

Conflict Managing Styles Questionnaire

1. **When you feel strongly about a conflict, you would:**
   ____ A. Enjoy the excitement and feel a sense of accomplishment.
   ____ B. View the conflict as a venture and a challenge.
   ____ C. Be concerned about how others are impacted.
   ____ D. Be dismayed because someone could be harmed.
   ____ E. Become persuaded there is little to anything you can do to resolve it.

2. **Ideally, what's the best result you expect from a conflict?**
   ____ A. It will encourage others to look at the issues and face facts.
   ____ B. It will eliminate extremes in positions and enable middle ground to surface.
   ____ C. It will clear the air, increasing commitment and results.
   ____ D. It will clarify the absurdity of a situation and draw co-workers closer together.
   ____ E. It will reduce complacency and apathy and identify who is to blame.

3. **When you have the final word in a conflict situation, you would:**
   ____ A. Let everyone know what your view is.
   ____ B. Attempt to negotiate the best settlement for all concerned.

_____ C. Encourage others to share their opinion and suggest that a position be found that both sides might try.

_____ D. Provide support to whatever the group decides.

_____ E. Remove yourself from the process, citing rules if they apply.

4. **If anyone is irrational, illogical, or unreasonable, you would:**

_____ A. Be blunt and say that you don't like it.

_____ B. Drop hints that you're not pleased; but avoid direct confrontation.

_____ C. Identify the conflict and suggest that you both probe possible solutions.

_____ D. Not say anything.

_____ E. Keep away from the person.

5. **When you become angry with a peer, you:**

_____ A. Rant and rave with little thought or concern.

_____ B. Try to gloss things over with a good story.

_____ C. Tell her you are angry and ask her for a response.

_____ D. Offset your anger by saying everything is OK, it wasn't a big deal.

_____ E. Withdraw yourself from the situation.

6. **If you disagree with co-workers about a project, you:**

_____ A. Hang firm and justify your position.

_____ B. Appeal to the logic and goodwill of the group in the hope of persuading most that your way or idea is the best.

____ C. Identify and review areas of agreement and disagreement, then look for options.

____ D. Give in and go with the group to keep the peace.

____ E. Withdraw from discussing the project and don't commit to any decision reached.

7. **When someone takes an opposite position to the rest of the team, you would:**

____ A. Tell the others in the group who the "roadblock" is and encourage them to move on without him or her if necessary.

____ B. Encourage her to communicate her objections so that a trade-off can be reached.

____ C. Learn why she views the issue differently so the others can re-evaluate their own positions.

____ D. Recommend the problem area be set aside and discuss other areas that are in agreement.

____ E. Keep quiet because it is best to not get involved.

8. **When conflict surfaces in your team, you:**

____ A. Press forward for a quick decision so the task gets completed.

____ B. Attempt to shift the dispute toward a middle ground.

____ C. Analyze the problem with the group so it can be discussed.

____ D. Relieve the tension with a good story.

____ E. If the conflict doesn't involve you, steer clear of it.

9. **In handling conflict between people, you would:**

_____ A. Anticipate areas of opposition and prepare replies to perceived objections prior to open conflicts.

_____ B. Encourage others to identify possible areas that may meet objections.

_____ C. Recognize that conflict does not mean disaster and encourage those involved to identify shared concerns and/or goals.

_____ D. Promote unanimity on the basis that the conflict can lead to the demise of friendly relations and friendships.

_____ E. Find someone who is neutral to arbitrate the matter.

10. **In your opinion, why would one group fail to work with another?**

_____ A. Lack of a clearly stated position or failure to back up and support the group's position.

_____ B. Tendency to force leaders to abide by the group's decision, as opposed to promoting flexibility, which could facilitate compromise.

_____ C. Tendency of groups to be myopic and view negotiations with a win/lose perspective.

_____ D. Lack of motivation to work peacefully with the other group.

_____ E. Leaders place emphasis on maintaining their own power versus addressing the issues involved.

Now, total the number of A's, B's, etc. and insert below:

A _____ B _____ C _____ D _____ E _____

Competing Compromising Collaborating Accommodating Avoiding

Source: The Briles Group, Inc. ©2001

Complete the survey in two ways. First, answer as you normally would as if you would under stress and pressure. After all, when you are in the midst of conflict, you most likely don't feel cool and calm. Next, make a shift. Where you see the personal pronouns relating to you, revise and substitute <u>she, her, he</u> or <u>him</u>.

For example: When <u>she has</u> (you) strong feelings in a conflict, <u>she</u> (you) would _____ .

(A) Enjoy the excitement and feel a sense of accomplishment.
(B) View the conflict as a venture and challenge.
(C) Be concerned about how others are impacted.
(D) Be dismayed because someone could be harmed.
(E) Be persuaded that there is little or nothing you can do to resolve it.

After you complete the exercise the second time around substituting she/he for you, you will then have a strong indication of another's style of dealing with conflict. Doing this puts you in the driver's seat. It gives you the opportunity to take the lead and adjust your style to match hers or his. When this happens, the person you are confronting will be better able to "hear" what you have to say. A compromise that allows for a more win-win result versus lose-lose.

Conflict-Handling Modes

Now, let's work with these five styles for handling conflict: competing, compromising, collaborating, accommodating, and avoiding, The grid below helps you identify your own way of handling conflict. Where do you fit?

The Five Conflict-Handling Modes

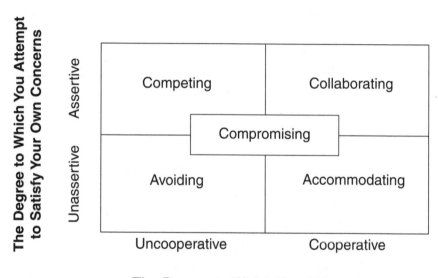

Source: Adapted from the Thoman-Kilmann Conflict Mode Instrument, developed by Kenneth W. Thoman and Ralph H. Kilmann in 1972. ("Mode" is an acronym for "Management of Differences Exercise.")

Assertive vs. Unassertive

Look at the side of the grid labeled *Assertive* and *Unassertive*. When you are unassertive, you want to pull back from a conflict, do anything to avoid a confrontation, make it go away. When you are assertive, you become more active in dealing with that conflict. If you speak up for what you believe in or what you perceive is justifiable, you are on the assertive side. If you believe that others routinely take advantage of you and that your voice isn't heard, you lean toward being non-assertive.

Cooperative vs. Uncooperative

Now, look at the cooperative style—the degree to which you attempt to satisfy someone's concerns. If you are a *Cooperative* person, you will do what you can to work with another, even when you don't agree. If you are the opposite—*Uncooperative*—your choice is either to avoid any dealings with him or her or attempt to resolve the issue your way.

Again, step back. If things don't go your way, have you ever felt or said, "I'm out of here?" Or do you say instead, "Hold on; let's continue to work and see if we can get to a resolution." The first approach is uncooperative; the second, cooperative.

By putting the two sides of the grid together, you see a matrix with five different styles of dealing with conflict. The compromising style is in the center. It represents the balance of being cooperative and uncooperative, assertive and unassertive. As you read the following descriptions, you'll recognize familiar ways to deal with conflict.

Meet the Styles

The five styles for handling conflict are explained below. Most likely, you use a combination of at least two. Each style has its own strengths and weaknesses.

The Competitive Style

Competitive women and men are very assertive. Getting their way is often at the top of their list; cooperating with others is secondary. They approach conflict in a direct and forceful way. Their attitude could be, "I don't care what other people think; it's my way or no way." Women and men who predominantly use the competitive style show more interest in satisfying their own concerns—often at the expense of others—and will do it by pulling rank, being forceful and/or arguing.

As an example, in the 1500s, Queen Elizabeth I ruled England with a firm hand. She surrounded herself as much as possible with submissive men. She was in charge, it was her game, she made the rules and others followed. If they didn't, they would meet their end, as Elizabeth's cousin Mary did.

The competitive style is a good style to have in your corner when you are in a position of power. It can alienate people, though. If you have little power (your position is weak and/or you have no support) in a situation and you use a competing style when disagreeing with someone you work with, you may find yourself without a job. Or, in a volunteer situation, a competitive style could alienate you from your committee members. Simply put, a competing style doesn't get desired results without power contacts and/or support behind you. Rather, competing styles work when you:

✓ Create win-lose situations;
✓ Use rivalry;
✓ Use power plays to get what you want;
✓ Force submission;
✓ Feel the issue is important and you have a big stake in getting your way;

✓ Have the power to make the decision; and it appears to be the best way to act;

✓ Must make a decision quickly and you have the power to make it;

✓ Feel you have no other options;

✓ Feel you have nothing to lose;

✓ Find yourself in an emergency situation requiring immediate, decisive action;

✓ Feel you are at an impasse requiring someone to make the group move ahead; or

✓ Have to make an unpopular decision, but action is required and you have the power to make that choice.

With a competitive style, your primary objective is not popularity. You may pick up supporters and admirers along the way if your solutions work. The style is used to get your way for something important to you. When you have to act immediately and are confident you will succeed, using a competitive style does not necessarily mean you are pushy.

When you confront a competitive person, it's a must to be direct and have your facts in order. Practice what you want to say. Any stumbles create a window to counter you.

The Collaborative Style

People who are collaborators get actively involved in working out any conflict. If your style is collaborative, you vocally assert what you want. At the same time, you also cooperate with others. Being collaborative takes time. It is not an instant "my way," as someone with a competitive style would demonstrate. Collaboration takes longer because you first have to identify the issues. Then each party must be willing to listen to the other's needs and concerns as well as other issues. If you have the time to process within the collaborating style, more probably a win-win scenario will evolve.

A collaborative style may initially surface when parties say their goals are the same. As you probe below the surface, other issues emerge which can lead to confusion about what the overall goal is. But this style works well when the parties involved have different underlying needs.

Let's say that a co-worker is consistently late and spends a lot of time during work hours doing personal business. Habitual lateness and misusing work time for personal business often are a front for other problems— feeling a lack of respect, acknowledgment, responsibility; the result is a disconnection with work in general, even boredom.

Cutting back personal phone use or keeping track of time spent doing personal items doesn't solve her problem. By doing that, initially it may look like it's been nipped in the bud. But the roots go deep. She may begin to act out in other ways. By actively listening, eliminating and dealing with obstacles she presents, you will move closer to your goal, though the problem won't be solved overnight.

When a collaborative approach is used, it often encourages each person at the table to identify their needs and wants . . . a key factor to a successful collaboration. When the issues are understood, it is far easier to seek alternatives and compromises that will work for all.

The collaborative style works when you:

✓ Are in a problem-solving position;
✓ Confront differences by sharing ideas and information;
✓ Search for integrated solutions;
✓ Find situations where all can win;
✓ See problems and conflicts as a challenge;

✓ Acknowledge the issues are important to both or all parties involved;

✓ Have a close, continuing or interdependent relationship with the other party;

✓ Set aside time to deal with the problem;

✓ Make sure you and the other person(s) are aware of the problem and are clear about what everyone wants;

✓ Show confidence the other party will put some thought and work into finding a solution with you;

✓ Possess the skills to articulate your concerns and listen to what others have to say; or

✓ Make sure others have a similar amount of power in a conflict, or will put aside any power differences to work together toward a solution as equals.

If those involved in a conflict will not agree to any of these elements, a collaborative style won't work. Because collaboration involves more time and commitment, it's more complicated. Yet if used successfully, it can be the most satisfying resolution for everyone, especially with a serious conflict.

The Accommodating Style

The person who uses the accommodating style likes to lend a hand and often easily conforms. It's a style that works on a cooperative basis with another without asserting one's own claim for power. When you have assessed a situation and decided it's a "no-win" for you, it makes sense to be accommodating. You might as well go along with whatever the other person wants. As an accommodator, you cede your own concern to the need to satisfy another's by sympathizing with that person or otherwise giving in.

When you invoke an accommodating style, you set aside your own concern; you feel you do not have a lot invested in the situation or the outcome. But if you feel that, in the end, you would be giving up something vital to you, then the accommodating style does not fit. It is also used to smooth things over for now so the issue can be brought up at a later time. This is viewed as a deferral, not avoidance, technique.

However, the accommodating style has some similarities to another style—avoiding. In the accommodating style, you willingly acknowledge the situation and agree to do whatever the other person wants to do. When avoidance is enforced, you do not do anything that will enhance the other's desires. A decision is reached more or less by default. It may be used to delay a final resolution.

Situations in which the accommodating style seem appropriate include:

✓ When you don't really care what happens in the end;
✓ When you want to keep peace and maintain harmony;
✓ When you feel like maintaining the relationship and avoiding anger;
✓ When you recognize that you are wrong;
✓ When you have minimal or no power;
✓ When you have no chance of winning;
✓ When you think the other person might learn from the situation if you go along with what he or she wants (even though you do not agree with what is being done);
✓ When you want a better position to be heard;
✓ When you want to learn more;
✓ When you want to show you are a team player;
✓ When you want to collect "chits" for later issues;
✓ Minimizing a loss when you are out-matched; or
✓ When outcomes or issues are not as important to you as to others.

When an environment is negative or hostile, you can often restore harmony by using an accommodating style to deal with a conflict. By sacrificing your concerns and yielding to what the other person wants, you may be able to smooth over a bad situation. The result allows you to use the period of calm as a method of gaining time. In the end, it enables you to work out a resolution you would prefer.

The Avoiding Style

Another major style, avoiding, occurs when you don't assert yourself, you don't cooperate or you avoid the conflict entirely. It's used when you feel you are in a "no-win" situation, you don't want to be a bothered or the whole problem is irrelevant. It is also used when you feel the other person is right, has more power, or you don't want to stick your neck out and take a position.

With this style, you sidestep and ignore the issue, delaying any input or decisions. It could also reflect that you don't have the time to deal with it now. Avoidance can work temporarily when dealing with someone who is difficult and you are not required to work together.

When you don't have to make a decision immediately, the avoiding style may do the trick. In reality, you choose to not make a decision. The "Catch 22" is that if you don't come back later to deal with the issue, others may view you as irresponsible or a procrastinator.

Avoidance also is effective when you have not been able to gather enough information to allow you to make a decision or recommendation. It enables you to be late with your input. If deferral is your objective, eventually you may have to come back and deal with the issue.

The avoiding style works well when you are:

✓ Ignoring conflicts or hoping they will go away;

✓ Putting problems under consideration on hold;

✓ Invoking slow procedures to stifle a conflict;

✓ Using secrecy to avoid confrontation;

✓ Appealing to bureaucratic rules as a source of conflict resolution;

✓ Needing to cool down tensions or back off;

✓ Knowing the issue is trivial to you;

✓ Having a bad day and not dealing rationally with the situation;

✓ Realizing you likely won't win or knowing you can't;

✓ Wanting more time, either to gather information or get help;

✓ Acknowledging the situation is complex and difficult to change;

✓ Feeling any time spent on the issue will be a waste of your time;

✓ Having little power to resolve the situation in a beneficial way;

✓ Feeling you aren't qualified to resolve the situation and others can do better;

✓ Aware that bringing the conflict into the open might make it worse; or

✓ Letting people cool down.

Many think that when people evoke an avoiding style in dealing with conflict, they are being evasive. At certain times, using delaying tactics is appropriate and can be constructive. Also, some conflicts do resolve themselves when given breathing room.

The Compromising Style

Located in the center of the matrix is the compromising/sharing approach. That means you give up a bit of what you want to get the rest of what you want. Other parties involved in the conflict do the same. A compromising solution is reached by using exchanges, concessions and bargaining that rarely satisfy everyone's concerns or objectives 100 percent. It will, though, meet the majority of concerns and objectives for each party.

In collaboration, you search for underlying needs and interests; in compromising, each person involved gives up some needs and/or interests before a resolution is reached. Let's say two of you have families and you both want to take off the first two weeks of July. You each have the same objective, yet only one can have vacation during that period. One of you will have to work unless the company decides to close its doors for a very long Independence Day holiday.

One compromise could be that one takes vacation this year and the other takes it next year. Who gets it first could be determined by the flip of a coin, seniority, work output, etc. Neither of you is assured of being 100 percent satisfied.

When collaborating, you focus on resolving various issues and needs, and it is marked by having differing needs. In the case of the July vacation, one worker may specifically need to be at a family reunion that's combined with a July 4th celebration while the others wants to see family but the timing isn't related to a scheduled event. When compromising, you recognize the conflict situation is a given, such as both parties having a scheduled event on July 4th. Often the goal in collaboration is a long-term, win-win solution. In a compromise situation, the outcome may more likely be short-term and expedient.

The compromising style works best when you are:

✓ Saving money;
✓ Conducting negotiations;

✓ Benefiting from a short-term gain;

✓ Looking for deals and trade-offs;

✓ Finding satisfactory or acceptable solutions;

✓ Wanting to achieve a resolution quickly;

✓ Collaborating or competing is unsuccessful;

✓ Settling for a temporary resolution to a complex issue;

✓ Modifying your goals because they are not important to you;

✓ Making the relationship or agreement work; it's better than nothing; or

✓ Coming from a place of equal power and being committed to mutually exclusive goals.

Use the compromising style when first stepping into the confrontation ring or when you don't have the power to get what you want. This way, you get part of what you want and the other party does too.

To be successful in compromising, it is important to clarify what are your needs and wants, as well as those of the other parties involved with the conflict. Then determine what areas you agree on. Once there is some agreement, a compromise settlement can be worked out. Listening is a critical part of the art of compromise.

Be willing to make suggestions and listen to what he or she says. In turn, the other party should be willing to do the same. Be prepared to give some things up—make offers and exchanges. It is imperative to identify areas that you won't budge on. The end result is that both of you should have some satisfaction with the outcome.

Which Style Is "You"?

Remember that there are times where a given style works best in a specific situation. Ideally, you should be able to recognize what styles are surfacing when dealing with another, as well as the styles you use to respond. As you become more skilled in dealing with conflicts, you will be able to consciously choose which style is most appropriate to use at a given time.

Look at the extremes. If you prefer the competitive or the avoidance style, you place yourself into a "win-lose" or "lose-lose" scenario. Restricting your style preferences limits you, though it's natural to prefer certain styles to others. Your first step is to determine your style preference in approaching conflict.

Usually, you have a dominant style followed by a secondary or back-up style. It's also possible that you have two equal characteristic styles such as avoidance and accommodation. A combination of these types indicates you prefer to prevent any type of conflict. When you have two equal characteristic styles, it's known as being *bimodal*. When you have three, it's *trimodal*. In most conflicts, it is normal to use your back up style first. If that doesn't work, then use all your power or strength . . . and make the transition to your dominant style.

You have just read about the five modes of conflict styles. Stop now and think for a moment. Which style best describes you? Did one stand out, or did you feel you were equally spread in your conflict styles? When you tallied your responses and identified your style, did it match the way you perceived yourself?

Sometimes it makes sense to use one style over another. The table below shows sample scenarios that *work* and *don't work* with each style.

Style	When it Works	When it Doesn't Work
Competing	• When you have the power	• When others don't respect your abilities or power
Accommodating	• When the other person requires status	• When you need a real solution
Avoiding	• When you must have the other person's participation	• When you have a lot to lose • When the other person is right
Collaborating	• When you have time; when you have a good relationship	• When there is a lack of trust • When time is short
Compromising	• When both are right • When you want to keep the relationship going	• When only one is right • When you have little to give

Keep in mind that conflicts are normal. What makes or breaks your circumstance is how they are handled.

In summing up, the styles can be identified as *competing* when you seek to get your own way; *collaborating* when you seek to work out a mutually satisfying solution with another; *accommodating* when you seek to work out an agreeable and satisfying solution with others; *avoiding* when you seek to avoid the conflict situation; *compromising* when you seek to work out a solution in which each party gives up a little to get some of what they want in return.

How To Carefront Effectively

In addition to determining your style, there are a few other techniques to use. The first is to identify a neutral area in which you can talk with the other person. Homes and offices of the respective parties are the wrong turf; neither of these can be considered neutral. Public areas where anyone can watch and listen are also inappropriate. Get a cup of coffee, tea, take a walk or find a quiet, isolated place where you can sit down one-on-one.

Before any confrontation, set some rules for yourself—for your own behavior. First, calm down. If you don't step back and take a moment to compose yourself, you could regret your words. Second, assess what's happened. View it from two sides: your perspective (what the impact and effect has been on you and if it has impacted others) and his/hers (what do you think their perspective is). Then take a deep breath. You need fresh oxygen in your system.

A key skill is your ability to listen; those who listen usually end up in control. As you listen, formulate the feedback you will give based on what you hear. Be willing to acknowledge that a behavior of yours may have been a factor in the conflict.

Commonly when one confronts another, don't be surprised when the response is denial. In fact, denying is more normal than not. *If* the actions and behaviors are denied, be prepared to back off. You have taken the first step. You have acknowledged that the behavior was not OK. The person responsible for the behavior likely knows it; few people are in total denial and cut off from the real world.

After you confront, drop it, let it go. It's time to move on. This does not mean you are to forget the actions and be all-forgiving. You are now alert. You now need to keep a watchful eye for any recurrences. If they do happen again, you confront again.

Changes rarely happen overnight. It will probably take a few confrontations to stop actions that negatively affect you or others. For many, confrontation is painfully uncomfortable. Yet each time you do it, it becomes less stressful. After all, you are learning a new behavior too. At some point, the light bulb turns on and those involved will realize their actions are destructive.

Talking with another face-to-face is usually the best way to confront. That way, she/he can see your body language and you can see hers/his. Some face-to-face confrontations require nerves of steel. That means you must be composed and have your facts together. Otherwise, emotions can erupt, and you either end up either attacking or retreating. At this point, the conflict only grows.

If meeting face-to-face is impossible, writing a letter becomes your second best choice. But this method has its drawbacks. For instance, you may not know whether your letter even gets read! Writing does, though, give you the opportunity to think out the facts as you understand them and clearly explain their impact and effect on you. Before sending any letters, have a trusted confidante read over your words to eliminate any inappropriate sharpness or over-emotional responses.

A less preferred way to confront is over the phone. This has several disadvantages. First, according to a well-known study by Dr. Albert Mehrabian of UCLA concerning one-on-one communication, 55 percent of the impact comes through gestures and body language. Face to face, you can visually see and react to what the other person is saying. Phone calls eliminate this aspect of communication. On the phone, also, you can't be sure that the other person is listening. In fact, she can put you on hold, walk away or even hang up before you are aware of it. Even if you both remain on the line, you cannot see each other's facial and body expressions. She/he is unable to visibly see your anger or hurt, but may hear it through your tone. Thirty-eight percent of communication comes from tone, something you *can* hear on the phone. The remaining seven percent come through words that are said. So you see, 93 percent of what is communicated is unspoken. Communication happens through seeing, feeling and interpreting.

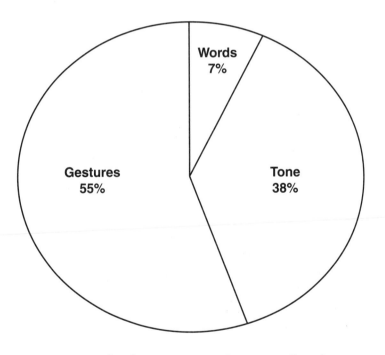

93% of what you say is unspoken!

Source: Dr. Albert Mehrabian, *Silent Messages* (Wadsworth Publishing, 1971)

Facing the Enemy

You may find yourself in a situation if you don't confront directly. You confront internally, within your mind, instead of confronting the person who needs it. You are practicing escapism, a variation of avoidance. Do you recognize yourself in any of these descriptions?

The Avoider

If your response to dealing with sticky circumstances is one of, "I'd rather be anywhere but here . . . ," you are an *avoider*. When it comes to confronting, *avoiders* are great prey for people who like to "steam roll" others. This stance rarely works.

The Complainer

Complainers would rather grumble, mumble or fume about a situation. Masters at internalizing, they operate under the mode that everyone around them is psychic. When friends and co-workers notice a change in attitude, they naturally inquire if something is wrong. But the response is usually, "No, nothing is wrong." Chronic *complainers* may actually enjoy being miserable and out of sync. They thrive on the attention they receive when others notice how miserable they are. It's part of the game.

The Could-Haves, Should-Haves and Ought-Tos

If you habitually respond either internally with a self-dialogue or to others with phrases that begin with *I could have, I should have* or *I ought to . . .* , you are a master at avoiding a situation.

Those who work in this sphere are like a VCR. They run their lives by putting in their "tapes" and pushing "rewind" to relive their misery. Then they come back with a strategy of *I could have, I should have* and *I ought to* and usually add on *". . . if only."* In their fantasy life, they come up with a reworked scenario that involves the confrontation . . . only it's said by the internal scriptwriter and never spoken out loud.

The Explosive

Explosives gather gnats that evolve into 2,000-pound gorillas. When their emotions erupt, often to a vocal extreme, those within the fallout distance are amazed how such a minor incident could trigger such a major eruption. But in most cases, a series of minor incidents led to the eruption. The old saying, "The straw that broke the camel's back" can be a perfect fit here.

When the *explosive's* fire dies down, debris falls everywhere. After a few eruptions, his apologies fall on deaf ears. Friends, colleagues and co-workers begin to distance themselves. Their attitude often becomes, "With friends like this, who needs enemies?"

Men and women who are in these groups—the *complainers*, the *could-have, should-have, ought tos*, and the *explosives*—have two things in common. First, they are on the path of avoidance; second, they are infused with an internal dialogue that says don't talk back or confront. They believe in maintaining their invisibility by remaining in the background . . . something no one can afford to practice in today's active world.

Your Personal Script

Getting the words out without stumbling always takes skill. I've put together a quasi-script for you to use to help get the process started. It goes like this . . .

> **When you** (What was the action?).
> **I felt** (What was your reaction?).
> **Because** (It looks like, sounds like, feels like.).
> **Was it your intent to** (What did he or she do?)?
> **In the future, I prefer** (How do you want him or her to act/respond from now on?).
> **If you don't, I will** (What's the consequence?)

   Let me give you an example. Let's say that George is a hog. He routinely takes credit for the work of others, including yours. Recently, he took credit for a project that you spent night and day on for six months to bring to completion.

> George, *when* you took credit for the project that I lead and just completed . . .
> I *felt* ticked . . .
> Because *it looked like* (feels like) you didn't want anyone to get recognition from our team, especially those of us who dropped everything and worked double shifts to bring it in ahead of schedule . . .
> Was it your intent *to not recognize and include me* in the successful completion of this major component of our team? (I need to add a critical factor here—**DO NOT, DO NOT, DO NOT answer your own question**—your silence is golden here . . . put the other person on the spot, almost forcing a response). . . .
> In the future, *I want* to be recognized and credited for the work that I do.
> If you don't, *I will* make sure that all the administrators are copied on the progress of future projects.

   People who take advantage of you are usually cowards and back down when you confront them. They also deny they did what you contend they did; or, they pretend that they didn't intend any harm, etc. The key is that you know what they did; they know that you know and you know that they know that you know!

JB's Keeper #7
If you don't confront an
inappropriate action, your silence says
it's OK to do it again . . . to you, and to others.

Self-Sabotage Flourishes Without Confrontation

There are several myths about anger and conflict. Many believe conflict means someone wants to take an advantage of another. Some believe a conflicting situation signals a lower concern from others. Many see anger as destructive while others say by leaving a conflict situation alone (avoidance technique!), it will go away. Still others insist all conflicts must be resolved, no matter what. Smile, shake hands, and let bygones be bygones!

All these myths are untrue. Conflicts arise because people have different goals and objectives; their perceptions vary; they hear differently; they come from different cultures, race and genders; general "noise"—news, events, happenings, fear and concerns—creates conflict. Most people call all this *life*.

Several predictable factors will escalate the tension around conflicts and confrontation. Normally, people in a conflict believe they know its cause *but* their analysis of the situation is usually inaccurate. Most conflicts are rooted in some type of action and intent. In reality, they are usually caused by a communication failure or breakdown, specifically in the listening area. Listening is an art—no one is born with a listening gene; it's a learned and practiced skill.

When you identify a situation in which you strongly believe another wants to physically, psychologically or professionally harm you, get out. You are better off gathering your marbles and finding another field to play in. Don't expect to change him or her . . . or their ways.

The need to be liked drives most human beings and contributes to almost every type of conflict. After all, people usually think if they don't win a point or a cause, then they lose. "If I lose, no one will like me." Who says?

If you are inclined toward "confrontophobia," you will do just about anything to avoid a confrontation. A lot of time can elapse. When a situation finally comes to a head, the original conflict may, by then, be an accumulation of half-remembered minor items.

When a lot of time has passed, non-resolution of a conflict becomes internalized. You tend to ask yourself, "What if I had done this?" or "What if I did that?" or "If only I hadn't let him get away with it," etc. You create a movie script in your head! Instead of a problem the size of a gnat, you are now dealing with the gorilla.

Learn how to handle conflicts in a reasonable and timely manner. When you understand your own conflict styles and those of others then take responsibility for your actions, everyone wins.

Final Thoughts on Confronting

Keep these key factors in mind when dealing with confrontations. First, recognize that conflict is not abnormal.

Conflicts arise daily from living and working with others. It is how you manage the conflict and confrontation that makes the difference.

Second, realize that the person in the confrontation who listens best usually wins. An expert listener listens with both eyes and ears, and pays close attention to the other person's words, tone, gestures and body language.

Third, using the other person's conflict style in your communication of the issues within the confrontation puts you ahead of the game. This takes practice, lots of it. It's a skill that is never learned overnight. You will find that in the beginning as you attempt to adapt, you will slip back to your usual style—your way. Just keep at it. Persevere—and you eventually will succeed in the transition from non-confrontive (where anyone can walk all over you) to carefrontive (you speak up and are not taken advantage of).

And fourth, document the facts of the issue, strictly the facts. That does not include an item-by-item account of your complaints. Documenting also enables you to get your thoughts in order as you record circumstances, dates and outcomes. If the other person is a master at getting you off track onto other topics, your documentation will give you the needed support to get back on your agenda.

Inevitably, you will address a series of conflicts throughout your life. Avoid them, and self-sabotage multiplies. More than that, you transition yourself into a victim mode, blame problems on others, create negative self-talk, procrastinate about future confrontations and reduce your confidence. This insidious chain of events holds you back. By learning to effectively confront one another, you can eliminate one of the most common ways you undermine yourself.

JB's Keeper #8
Conflicts that are piddles and
not addressed can turn into puddles,
ponds and torrential rivers.
You end up drowning.

Chapter Seven

 Egomaniac Alert—
Are You SO Important?

Valuing your worth and your importance is critical in building self-esteem and confidence. But some people develop an inflated sense of self-worth—or believe they accomplish the same thing by constantly devaluing the worth of others. Commonly, a person with an over-inflated ego grabs the spotlight whenever possible. And it's usually to the detriment of others.

Egomaniacs abhor seeing someone else shine or receive accolades. Thus they usually find a way to muscle in. Don't be surprised if you hear some of them take credit for work that's being rewarded; they could even claim credit for the initial genius behind the success.

Men and women with bloated egos are usually bullies who lack confidence, but they often get where/what they want (they win!) because no one will confront them. Real confidence, on the other hand, is the power you give yourself. It comes from a solid value system that includes the caring and self-worth you have for yourself. An ego-maniac's show of confidence is a clever impostor of the real thing. Those with bulging egos view themselves as the *key and only central figure* with their co-workers, with their families and in their circle of friends—if they have any.

They are absolutely never wrong and will argue to the death on how right they are. Failure is never a possibility in the minds of those with inflated egos. But when they do fail, they will not acknowledge or accept their own part in the failure to themselves or anyone else. And so, those with over-inflated egos proficiently lay blame on other people or on uncontrollable events for anything that isn't perfect in their lives. Mega egos are a pain in the tush.

We Are So Important

I read a lot wherever I am. Because I travel frequently, I often scan a minimum of three newspapers on any given day—*USA Today, The Wall Street Journal,* and the major newspaper of the city I am in. Business and family magazines are added to my weekly reading pile—*Time, Newsweek, Inc., Fast Company,* sometimes *Fortune, Inc.* or *Forbes, Money, Bloomberg Financial* and, yes, even *People* and *TV Guide.* I try to catch all the news—business, entertainment, world events, and, of course, gossip.

Each day presents pages of startling, stunning and sometimes boring information. It includes features on celebrities and wannabe celebrities. Let's consider two featured celebrities: "The Donald" as in Donald Trump and the Queen of Hotels, Leona Helmsley. Both made headlines in the last decade. Both have egos—huge egos.

Helmsley showcased hers in a series of high profile, expensive full-page ads in national magazines and television spots. The glitz conveyed the message that, because she is in charge, you would be treated royally at her hotels. You could expect to be the Queen or King during your stay under her roof.

She delivered what she promised and her standards were respected by the most knowledgeable. Helmsley personally inspected plates of salad to make sure that a drop of water doesn't dilute the dressing or a wilted leaf isn't found on the plate. (As an aside, she even commissioned a designer to develop a deck of cards that had her face, as Queen, featured within the deck. If you asked for playing cards at her hotels, you got Leona Helmsley's cards.)

The Donald made a bigger splash than Leona Helmsley did. *His* picture graced the jackets of several books he authored (most likely with a great deal of assistance from a ghostwriter), including his first New York Times bestseller *The Art of the Deal.* Trump Towers in New York City and two casinos in Atlantic City, New Jersey, bear his moniker. These show places attract tourists just because of their opulence.

Both Helmsley's and Trump's egos soared stratospheres above the average person's for a long time without a hitch. But both have faced financial difficulties. Trump defaulted on some loans and had real estate deals that didn't work out. No one could miss his well-publicized divorce from first wife Ivana and remarriage to (now divorced) second wife Marla. He paid out a lot to both of these women.

Helmsley overstepped the rules for allowable business deductions, resulting in the highly visible IRS trial that sent her to prison for tax avoidance. It's probably a fair assumption to say their egos soared so high, they were blinded by the sunlight that shined on them. Or maybe they felt they were untouchable; they had become convinced that the world revolved around them and them alone.

Donald Trump and Leona Helmsley have paid (and continue to pay) enormous amounts of money every month to public relations firms who enhance their business endeavors and probably feed their gluttonous egos. During the very public Trump divorce, both parties had their own PR firms. Very few people knew much about Ivana previously, but we didn't have to look far or long for the PR statements extolling how wonderful they each were. The publicity folks also handled damage control when needed, and they had a big job sweeping up the dirt.

Helmsley left her prison cell in the fall of 1994. Did the experience clip the wings of her ego? Today, when you see advertisements for various Helmsley hotels, her "on camera" participation is missing. Has she totally disappeared? No. The lead line in a recent airline magazine ad is: "She Knows People Talk About Her. She'll Even Show You What They Say." The final tag line was, "We promise it'll receive the personal attention of You-Know-Who." She's out there, just a tad more subtle! Sounds like she learned to capitalize on her experiences, too.

Nothing Could Get Done Without You

Are inflated egos exclusive to celebrities? Absolutely not. An expanded ego can park on anyone's doorstep. Egotistic celebrities and their less famous brethren share common traits. Individuals with hefty egos believe—truly believe—they are indispensable. In some cases, their persona and talents would be missed if they were gone. Most, however, can be replaced. In fact, a replacement would be welcomed with a resounding sigh of relief.

Though none of us is indispensable, events can make us think we are. Focusing on what is really important sometimes gets lost when the limelight is ours. Ego food is fine dining but it can leave a bitter taste in the mouths of our staunchest supporters—friends, family and co-workers. George can attest to this.

George lives and works in a medium size mid-west city. He's married with two kids and has taken great pride in his community involvement. For several years, he's donated many hours to an annual Chamber of Commerce conference that focused on women. The event was for women of all definitions—women who worked for a paycheck, women who were moms and grandmas, women who were old and young, single and married.

The conference was organized by a board that consisted of representatives from all the men's and women's clubs and associations in his city. For the person who chaired the event, it was comparable to holding a full time job. George was thrilled and quite proud when he was elected chair for the conference. He told his story this way,

> For years, I had worked on committees, climbing the different committee chair ladders until I reached the top. We routinely have 1,000 to 1,500 women in attendance, so it's a big event for our community.
>
> Media interest is so broad that, unless a major news story breaks, coverage for our two-day conference dominates the radio, local TV, and newspaper. The wife of the publisher of the local paper sits on our board, so it's guaranteed the conference is highlighted.
>
> I knew there would be tons of work when I became chair so I forewarned my family they wouldn't see much of me a few months before the conference and not at all the week of it. When I told my co-workers I would be tied up with a lot of committee meetings, I asked them to help me out. Well, maybe I didn't really ask them; it was more

like telling them—at least, that's what they said after the conference was over.

I reasoned that, with all the publicity and the goodwill that came from the event, surely it would make everyone feel good that our company—because of my work—was involved. I knew my name would be used everywhere and it was, it would be great publicity for my company—all free!

My favorite part was the publicity. I loved the radio and TV spotlight and being interviewed for newspaper articles. My picture was everywhere. I even touched my hair up before I did a public service spot for a local station!

I worked so incredibly hard beforehand, there were days I didn't know where I was. The weekend of the conference, I checked into the hotel next to the convention center to be available to anyone at anytime. The conference was a huge success!

But in looking back, I had assumed support would come from my family, friends and co-workers. I was irritated that it just wasn't there. And if there were clues, I didn't see them coming. I thought everyone supported me.

Yes, the conference was great. I wasn't. By the time it was over, my name was mud with a lot of people I cared about. My wife asked me who I was; my friends avoided me saying that they didn't think they mattered; my co-workers refused to cover for all my absences prior to and during the conference.

I was so obsessed with being Mr. Conference, I forgot why I got involved in the first place. I took advantage of everyone in my circle. I felt nothing would be done right unless I was there. Being seen and heard became very important. My ego was totally out of control.

It took awhile for George to repair and rebuild some of the fences he had stomped on. His forgiving family was glad to see him back—physically and in spirit. His true friends hung in there. Others weren't so kind. One former friend told him if he had wanted to be in an abusive relationship, he would return to his alcoholic ex-wife.

His co-workers took him to lunch one day and vented. At first, George denied he had been away from his work as much as they claimed. An exasperated co-worker got out a list that detailed tasks they had done for him while he continued to collect a paycheck.

George was embarrassed and angry. At them and at himself. When he asked why no one spoke up sooner, in unison they said they had! He chose not to listen. George did pick up the lunch tab that day, but it took a full year to make amends to his co-workers.

The Phone's For Whom?

I spend a lot of time in airports and on airplanes. Over the past two years, I've noticed a significant intrusion of noise in my space and my seatmate's space. What kind of noise? Simply this: the telephone.

Because my airline seat often becomes my office, I need more than the incredibly crunched-up environment which coach seats force on any flyer. Whether it's writing on the computer, editing hard copy or just stretching my legs, I often upgrade to a business or first class seat, which offers more comfort and work room.

Today's planes, especially in business and first class, have a telephone at each seat. Airlines encourage flyers at check-in to receive a "private" number so they can take calls during the flight. Now, include all the cell phones!

Flyers like me don't need to be forced to hear the conversations of someone across the row, beside me, or in front or back. Yes, I know most business people travel during regular hours. But today, few flights last much longer than three hours and most are shorter. Unless you are president of the United States or a major company (they all have their own private jets anyway), are you so incredibly important you need a phone in your hands every minute? I don't think so.

I am forced to listen to dozens of conversations . . . word for word. There are two types—one basically is nonsense such as, "Hey I'm flying in a DC 10 on my way to Hawaii. You should have seen what they served for lunch. Blab, blab, blab." I wasn't the lone listener; 20 other passengers heard this guy loudly gab about nothing.

Other conversations have involved details of business deals that border on revealing privileged information. If I had been a competitor of the company being discussed, I would use that inside information to my advantage. Anyone using an air phone is compelled to speak far more loudly than a normal voice—those engines are noisy!

At hotels, including nice resorts, men and women have phones stuck to their ears. It doesn't matter if they are eating breakfast, lunch or dinner. They are so important that they can't take 30 minutes to enjoy a meal—or allow those around them to enjoy theirs— without broadcasting their one-way conversation in a loud voice. What gives?

The telephone is a marvelous instrument. But let's get real and get balanced. Some people use them as an aid. Many, and the number is a growing number according to my observations, use them as a status "I am so important" symbol. Don't. It's OK to leave home without your phone.

At the very least, let others enjoy some peace and quiet, even if you can't!

The Renaissance Women

Speaking of balance, one of the things I do on a monthly basis is get together with four very trusted women friends over a potluck dinner. We all come from different walks of life, have a 15-year age range, and work at different occupations. We call ourselves The Renaissance Women.

Two of us are married, one never has been married, and the other was divorced several years ago. We have incredible similarities . . . and a wide range of differences.

We have become a support group for each other—both professionally and personally. We share hopes, fears, dreams, triumphs, and failures. Most importantly, we are *a reality check* for each other. If, at any time, one of us feels that another is too heady, too pushy, or not being realistic—anything that's a concern—the issue gets put on the dinner table for discussion.

I would encourage you to create a support group like mine. My friends serve as my advisory board and I care for them deeply. It took awhile to get to our "four." Even scheduling monthly has been a challenge at times, especially with two of us traveling extensively.

Other women have participated at different times over the past six years. For a variety of reasons (commitment, time, even the wrong fit), they aren't included any longer. You may be thinking, "It's not nice to exclude someone." I will disagree.

If you are sharing your deepest hopes, dreams, fears, and concerns, and someone misuses the information you share, a crevice is introduced into your group. It could be a crevice that runs so deep, it can split the group.

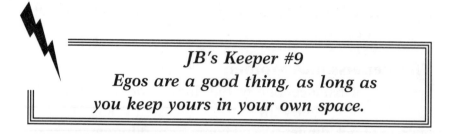

JB's Keeper #9
Egos are a good thing, as long as you keep yours in your own space.

We all have egos. The issue here is to keep them in balance—and doing it for yourself is hard. Imagine riding a teeter-totter with its continual ups and downs. Egos are like that, too—they go up and down. When you can confide in a trusted friend, your ups and downs are more likely to even out, and you'll stay in balance.

Chapter Eight

 Paranoia—How Could
Everyone Be Against You?

Have you ever felt that the world was against you? If not the world, how about the people you work with? Or even family members? Most likely, they aren't. Few are really against you; it just feels that way at times. Usually, those times surface when you are vulnerable. When you feel alone or are new to a situation—workplace, neighborhood or community—you can easily feel that no one likes or wants you. After all, who has had the opportunity to really get to know you?

My childhood family didn't feel like the family life I experience today. My parents were quite remote. I always thought they should have raised four-legged animals instead of my three brothers and myself. In reality, we didn't see that much of our parents. My father worked all the time my mother was indifferent. I moved out when I was 16 to start a life and family of my own.

When I was seven years old, my parents moved from Los Angeles to a beach community—one of the dozens of moves we made during my growing-up years. I felt so lonely in a new city and new school; friendships were always hard to build. As the "new girl" I was the butt of jokes and pranks . . . at least, that's the way I felt back then. We never stayed in one place very long before the moving van came again.

As a seven-year-old in my new neighborhood, I saw few kids out playing, so when I finally met another girl my age, I was ecstatic. Diane even had three sisters—what a bonus!

I "adopted" her family—my first "heart" family. I spent every waking, and sleeping, moment in the Wilkinson household. I discovered parents who like their kids; have fun with them; teach and guide them; love them. Whoa— what an exciting revelation to a young girl hungry for someone to recognize that she had some value.

Each time we moved, I thought no one liked me. My parents had cautioned us kids to not tell anyone about our family or what my father did. (I didn't have a clue what he did until I was an adult. I learned he had worked in the defense industry in what would be called human resources today. He eventually tried to run a company that made military equipment. It failed.) "It's nobody's business," I remember my mother warning. As adults, my brothers and I concluded they always kept one step ahead of the bill collectors. That's why we never threw away our moving boxes and never told old neighbors our new phone number!

Fortunately, I learned at the early age of seven to override my parents' rejection by seeking support from other sources. In my case, it was a new family like the Wilkinsons. When I was twelve, I adopted my second "heart" family. A few years later, in fact, I married into it! Joyce, my mother-in-law, is the mom every child should be blessed to have. Until I connected with her, though, that isolation and loneliness I felt had become a form of paranoia. I truly believed no one liked me, that no one wanted me.

Recognizing Paranoia

If you have ever been around people who are paranoid, you know they believe the world is out to get them. They are suspicious of just about everything and everyone around them. If you are paranoid, you are distracted from your work. Your energy and creativity are used up by a variety of manifestations. You honestly believe others want to destroy your work or reputation and discredit your capabilities.

You feel enclosed in a glass box. You want to look out and see what is going on. At the same time, you isolate yourself from everyone who might "get you" or think badly of you. Some possibly familiar examples follow.

It's My Fault

Paranoia is often a creature birthed from self-doubt. As a school administrator, Harold had to routinely catch himself when self-doubt surfaced. He told his story this way,

> It is common to have teaching assistants within our school. Part of my job is to evaluate their skills and train them. Sometimes, it's very easy. I know immediately if they are on the ball and, when they are, I have few problems with them.
>
> But when someone isn't doing well and can't follow instructions, I would begin to believe it was my fault. I would start to say, 'Is it me; am I expecting too much; am I being too hard on this new assistant?'

Pretty soon, I would begin to mistrust my own judgment and hurt my ability to do my job well. Those self-doubts are so strong, they can make me paranoid.

A Gift of Tea

Marsha usually takes her three-year-old twins to day care twice a week for some well-deserved "mom's time out."

Usually, the care provider, Kay, greets her and the twins enthusiastically when they arrive. During one visit, though, Marsha felt that she was being snubbed when she dropped the kids off. Though Kay had been friendly in the past, Marsha barely got a hello or smile from her.

Marsha began to feel she wasn't liked. She racked her brain to figure out what she (or her kids) had done to offend Kay. Maybe Marsha wasn't being as pleasant as she could be; maybe she had been rude or said something to hurt Kay's feelings; maybe . . .

After agonizing over the issue for awhile, Marsha asked her husband if he had noticed anything unusual when he picked the twins up the previous week. He said no, that the kids were glad to see him, and they hugged everyone as they left. Marsha then shared her feelings and doubts. She felt that somehow she had made a mistake or done something to turn Kay away from her.

Her husband then offered some savvy advice: "Why don't you call Kay about that or ask her the next time you see her? It doesn't make sense to think she doesn't like you. Maybe she's had some problems in her family. Have you asked any other parents if Kay seems distant lately?"

Marsha thought about his advice for a few days. When she dropped off the twins the following Monday, she brought a tin of her favorite tea with her. As she took off her kids' coats, she said, "The twins love coming here. Last time I dropped them off, I felt you were feeling overwhelmed, so I brought you some of my favorite tea. I thought it might help and that you would enjoy it."

Giving the tea was just what the doctor ordered. Kay's whole face smiled. "Thank you. I need something nice right now. My favorite brother was diagnosed with terminal cancer last month. It's been so hard just getting through each day."

This response caught Marsha off guard. She was so sure she had said or done something wrong, she never imagined another factor caused the care provider's shift in attitude. Marsha had let her self-doubts stop her from being rationale or stepping back to see if there could be reasons other than the emotional "she doesn't like me."

Not In Our Neighborhood

Neighborhoods are mini-cities in a way. Many women, and men, operate businesses out of their homes. Most self-employed women start companies under their own roofs—anything ranging from authoring and speaking (as I have been doing full time since 1986) to consumer-oriented activities to light manufacturing.

Sometimes company owners or people who work for them don't mesh well with neighbors. Georgia found herself caught in the middle of such a quasi-feud. She runs a home-based business that specializes in bookkeeping for small companies. The neighbor Susan, who lives directly across the street, also operates a home-based business. She designs and manufactures hats.

Georgia's problem started with the issue of the garage door. One Saturday morning, the cul-de-sac where they lived was filled with vibrating noises of industrial sewing machines. Her husband Thomas decided the noise level was just too high. And both were irritated that they had to look at their neighbor's open garage door from 7 a.m. until late at night. Why? Because the heat of the summer, coupled with the noise of the machines, made it difficult for the seamstresses to work with the garage door closed.

Thomas decided to handle the problem by contacting their homeowners' association. Within the covenants were rules about home-based businesses. The constant noise, large machinery, and leaving the garage door up continuously violated the covenants.

Within a few days, Georgia and Thomas received a phone call, then a threat. Their enterprising neighbors had figured out where the complaint came from. Before they could say, "there must be a misunderstanding," war was declared. Susan's husband John threatened to punch Thomas in the nose. Two neighbors who knew both women told Georgia it was all her fault that Susan was going to lose her business. Georgia was afraid the situation would get out of hand. She explained her reaction this way,

> I began to believe no one likes me . . . likes us. I dreamt I got phone calls from neighbors late at night accusing me of spreading gossip, being unkind to their kids, being mean to Susan and not supporting her business. You name it, in my mind I have been called it and accused of it. I came to expect more criticism every time the phone rings.
>
> These feelings are ridiculous. I'm all for small businesses and I think it's great to work out of the home. But Susan and John have chosen to create a business that violates neighborhood peace and quiet. It directly violates our rules. We bit our tongues for a year

before we finally spoke up. Now, I'm afraid of rejection from our neighbors as well as them. It feels like it doesn't matter what we do or say, no one likes us.

Remedies at Hand

Wherever you are today, if paranoia is one of the snares you find yourself in, take an active role in eliminating it. Often the bark is worse than the bite. When paranoia is your partner, it is common to exaggerate issues and concerns. The childhood ditty mentioned in the first chapter,

> No one loves me,
> everybody hates me,
> think I'll eat some worms . . .

is your working hymn.

To overcome feelings of paranoia, you can work them through and be much more proactive than Georgia, Marsha, and Harold were in the examples above. Concentrate on these six areas to reduce—and eventually eliminate—your paranoia (so you can sing a happier tune than the worm ditty):

1. ***Don't be so harsh on yourself.*** Stop being your own worst enemy. Everyone makes mistakes, blows it. Few people really dislike someone because of an error or blunder. After all, you are human, aren't you?
2. ***Stop treating yourself, or believing that you treat yourself, unfairly.*** Granted, there are going to be people out there—family, co-workers, even "friends"—who wouldn't mind if you looked foolish once in a while.
3. ***Be accurate with the words you use.*** "Always," "everyone," and "never" are frequently used as gener-

alizations which add to feelings of paranoia. It's highly unlikely that *"Everyone* is mad at me," or "I *always* flub up," or "I can *never* win," or *"Everyone* hates me."

4. ***Get feedback from someone you trust.*** Your concerns that neighbors, co-workers, or others want to "do you in" may be misinterpreted or exaggerated. Sometimes, the voice of someone who is not involved generates an excellent reality check.

   In Georgia's case, she followed this advice and talked with women in her daughter's playgroup. It turned out one of them knew Susan and John's former neighbors. They reported a similar situation occurred with the couple in the last neighborhood they lived in!

5. ***Don't take everything so personally.*** Whether it's with a questionable tone or critique from a spouse, friend, coworker or a boss, it's not uncommon to "read" more in to it than what "it" really is. If you are unsure, clarify—sometimes talking with another person helps to bounce your concern off— instead of brewing.

   In Marsha's case, she imagined all kinds of reason's why Kay was giving her the cold shoulder, letting her perceived "I don't like you anymore" snubbing from Kay take over her common sense. She began to believe that she must have done something to initiate the rude and distant interaction from Kay. She let the "maybes" take over, never thinking that Kay might have been under extreme stress from issues totally unrelated to her. Marsha's husband encouraged her just to ask. She did, and learned that Kay's favorite brother was dying.

6. ***Seek some professional help.*** If you feel you can't

trust anyone in your immediate circle, then seek help. At work, turn to a respected department head or manager, or a professional counselor in the human resource department or in your community. If you are deeply distrustful—believing everyone dislikes you and wants you to fail—you might require the help of a trained therapist. Seek one out. *The one thing you should not do is nothing*.

Most self-sabotaging behaviors, paranoia for one, are self-feeding—the longer you allow them in your life, the stronger their hold on you. In time, you will lose any semblance of control over your experiences.

JB's Keeper #10
Paranoia is usually self-imposed—
that acknowledgment is the first step
toward removing it from your bag of snares.

Chapter Nine

 Fairness—
Life Isn't Always Just

A story from my book *When God Says NO* depicts my six-year-old son sitting on the curb with a neighbor boy, both waiting for a school bus. Now, I don't remember if my son neglected to eat his breakfast or if he was just bored, but when I spied him, he was wolfing down the peanut butter sandwich I had packed for his lunch. After polishing off his sandwich, Frank and his school chum crossed the street and came into the house. In unison they announced, "We've quit school. It's too long, too hard and not fair." Believe me, those words were not thrilling to my ears. While I made fresh sandwiches for both boys, I decided on the appropriate response to their ultimatum. In my best "kick 'em in the pants voice" I said, "Life is often too long, too hard and unfair. Take these sandwiches, boys, and march out to wait for your bus. NOW."

Ahhh, wouldn't we all love to live in a world that was

always fair and just? Well it's not and we're not living in one that is. Dealing with the variety of injustices and circumstances in everyday life requires a strong middle-of-the-road position. It's attitude that counts—Pollyannas and skeptics are both ill-equipped to deal with the cards in an unfairness hand when it comes their way. Failure to deal appropriately with unfairness is another form of self-sabotage.

Getting a Fair Deal?

Recently, I took a late night phone call from a friend of many years. Sid, my friend, had just learned that his job as the national director of sales for a healthcare organization had ended. Two weeks before, his employer announced it had been bought by a multi-billion dollar Fortune 100 company . . . not an unusual occurrence in the past decade. But his emotions were running the gamut as we talked.

Sid felt he had been betrayed. He sounded bewildered as he recounted what he had lost, including moving his family from one coast to the other. Because he couldn't afford mortgages on two homes, he suffered a huge loss on the forced sale of his house in a depressed real estate market.

"A complete waste," he concluded about the last six years of his life . . . overlooking his accomplishments. During that time, he had tripled sales—a feat that probably made his company an attractive buy-out candidate. His activities clearly helped the company grow. During the past year, in fact, his good efforts beat out the acquiring company in several competitive bid situations. He was incensed! Where was the loyalty, the recognition of all the creative work that he had done? Sid couldn't believe that he, of all people, was now among the unemployed. He fumed,

I don't know which of the following gets to me more. The owners walked away with in excess of 100 million dollars in their pockets, due in part to all the work my team did to create value in the company. My severance package was totally out of sync with what other healthcare companies offered key people in mergers and acquisitions. I only received two months of my annual income. At the very least, I should have been included in the package as a consultant during a transition period.

I'm angry about how I was treated and about how our entire sales force was treated. Out of 44 sales positions, only 10 were retained—the rest received a one-week severance for each year of employment, including vacation time. Managers in the acquiring company reasoned that they wanted to use their own sales force.

The buying company offered a hardship safety net: if an ex-employee exhausted all savings including pension funds and still hadn't found employment, he or she could apply to the company for additional monies. Employment at the same level as the one lost apparently wasn't what they meant; some reps were told if employment became difficult, they could always apply at McDonald's. It's not fair.

Sid told me he planned to write to the chairman of the board of the acquiring company. He intended to appeal to his sense of fairness.

Sid missed the clues that a buy-out was coming, so time was of the essence when he got his two-week notice. For Sid, this meant identifying how he would fit into the new scheme of things, what he wanted and what he could compromise on. This done, he needed to find the appropriate ears in both groups: the acquiring company and his present company. He had to aggressively get the word out, while emphasizing his willingness to be cooperative.

Unfortunately, Sid wasn't aggressive because he didn't think he had to be. Instead, he believed that justice would be delivered, and that his good track record and reputation would make him indispensable to the acquiring company. Mostly, he believed all parties would be fair.

Did you ever hear, "All good things come to those who wait?" Another myth or Momism—life is rarely fair. You can increase the odds of fair treatment by speaking up and speaking out. Since Sid didn't, writing to the chairman could be viewed as sour grapes. His actions may actually be "cooking his goose" in the new job marketplace. Why? Word of his letter to the chairman could get around. He could then be viewed as demanding, non-supportive and not a team player—not worth bothering with. His job now is to go forward and use this extremely painful experience as a tool for growth.

When Friends Leave You Out on a Limb

Every fall I organize an annual cruise. It's called the Confidence Cruise. Participants attend workshops during the morning hours then enjoy shipboard and land activities in the afternoons and the evenings.

Charissa, a department manager for a hospital on the East Coast, was one of the participants in this year's Confidence Cruise. At the workshop covering Women Managing Women, she shared that she was dreading her return to work at the hospital next week. She had a very unpleasant task at the top of her to do list—fire her subordinate Suzanne. She explained,

It's not fair. Suzanne has been my friend for several years. When I was made manager of the department, I became her boss, too. The past year has been difficult for her. She's recently gone through a divorce, one of her kids has MS and, on top of that, Suzanne has a health problem the doctors haven't been able to diagnose—so far the tests have been inconclusive.

I have done everything I can to offer her flexibility in meeting her work requirements, so that she can meet her personal obligations. My heart really goes out to her. But she continues to be erratic—she doesn't get to work on time, doesn't complete assignments, and needs lots of extra time away from our department for the various lab tests the doctors keep requesting.

Three months ago, my administrator warned me that I had to put Suzanne on probation, and I did. I know Suzanne needs her job, so I did my best to communicate to her the necessity of getting to work on time and reducing the number of hours away from our department. Last week, the administrator declared that Suzanne has got to go. And I get the honors of telling her that she's fired.

Because she really needs all the help she can get, my "friend" side says I should give Suzanne another chance. I know that when the doctors find out what's wrong with her and her son stabilizes, she will be in on time and start getting her work done. I know that, in the past, others in our department enjoyed working with her. Recently, though, staff members have complained to my boss that they are tired of picking up her share of the load. Somehow it just doesn't seem to be fair. To her. Or to me.

Charissa let her personal feelings for her friend blind her and she put herself in a "Catch 22" position. She hasn't made a clear distinction between being a boss and a friend to Suzanne. While her friend certainly deserves compassion and sympathy when traveling a rocky road, Charissa still has a job that needs to be done.

Charissa knows that Suzanne has been given enough chances, she hasn't performed and the only choice is to terminate her. Still, it didn't seem fair. She felt she was betraying their friendship.

During the workshop discussion, the other participants told Charissa she had not dealt with Suzanne in an effective or timely manner, thus respect for her as a manager was on the decline. I referred her back to the Friendship Friendliness Quiz that is displayed in Chapter Five.

As unfair as it seemed, the only choice for Charissa was to terminate Suzanne. The sooner the better. Charissa had a distorted sense of fairness and it interfered with her effectiveness as a manager, contributing to a form of self-sabotage.

Don't Be the Rescuer

Most of us know of someone whose boss routinely delivers a barrage of "must have immediately" work. And that work must be completed by the end of the day or first thing in the morning. Unfortunately the work usually isn't delivered until shortly before quitting time. People with bosses like this seem to be unable to say no. But if you ask if they like the long hours, they tell you absolutely not. They complain that the boss always takes advantage of them.

Melanie, another of this year's cruisers has worked as an executive secretary for 15 years. She takes great pride in the quality and amount of work she can produce in a short time. George, Melanie's primary boss, is a master procrastinator. His project deadlines are always only a few hours away. Here's what Melanie said,

> I hate working all the extra hours that George piles up for me. My eyes and wrists hurt because of the hours I spend in front of the computer. George always gives me reports to complete at the last minute. If I don't get them done, his neck will be in a noose.
>
> One of the women in the department tried to take me under her wing. She gave me a book about speaking up and being assertive. She constantly told me to tell George "no"—he needs to get his project reports to me earlier in the day. I'd love to read the book, but I'm just too busy. And, the truth of the matter is, I'm afraid to say anything to George. I know that my family would like me to get home at a decent hour. I just don't know what to do.

In a case like Melanie's, other people in an office are likely to take note of what's going on and become involved. Why? They reason that if poor Melanie can't speak up, then someone's got to do it for her. Poor baby! They feel it's not fair she has to work so hard and is never appreciated. If George is approached directly about the unfairness of Melanie's situation, he will probably ignore it, or he will say it's none of anyone else's business. And, he would be justified in saying that. After all, if Melanie is concerned, she can come directly to him and discuss it. Poor, poor Melanie!

When you take unfairness in hand and decide to "champion" for another, you may see yourself as that person's hero, which may not be the case. Speaking up on behalf of the Melanies in the world reinforces their inability to speak up for themselves. And, you could damage your own re-putation—become known as someone who interferes un-necessarily. This is another way an expectation of fairness shows up and contributes to self-sabotaging behavior.

What was our collective Confidence Cruise advice to Melanie? Continue the good work—she had taken the first step in helping herself by joining us on the cruise. Take a course on assertiveness. Even role play with others so she could practice speaking up, not only to her boss but to her co-workers who see her boss' behavior as unfair. Don't expect others to rescue her.

Not all advice is the right advice, or good advice. Another friend suggested she should transfer to another department. Will that resolve Melanie's problems? Prob-ably not. Until she learns to fight her own battles, the Georges of the world will continue to dominate and mis-use her. She will never feel like she gets a fair deal in her work life. Granted, it's not fair but it's life.

Dealing With Fairness

Is getting a fair deal simply a game of roulette? Certainly not. You can increase your odds considerably by concen-trating on the following:

✓ Don't assume anything.
✓ Be assertive.
✓ Decide, for yourself, which battles to take on.
✓ Speak up and speak out.
✓ Be impartial and unbiased.
✓ Recognize what works for one might not be a fit for another.
✓ Develop a strong value system. Don't ask another to do something you wouldn't do yourself.

✓ Make rules for your relationships with friends, family or co-workers. Then be consistent and predictable in their use.

The ability or inability to identify fairness may come from some *Momisms* you grew up with. Be Fair. Share. Be Patient. Don't Brag. How does bragging fit in with this? Simply put, if life was fair, if the workplace was fair, if relationships were fair, you would not have to take credit for work you have done—or shout your own bravos. Everyone would know about the many great things you do. That would be the fair thing in a totally fair world!

Not everyone does know, of course. How many who need recognition are featured on the nightly news or on the front section of the newspaper? Most likely, no source shouts out your accomplishments. That is, no source except you. The world is filled with millions of unsung heroes and heroines, and you are probably one of them.

Most men can brag about themselves with ease, so let's do something for the cause of equality in bragging. If you're in favor, just jump up on the box and say, "Hey, look at me. I'm great, I'm wonderful, I deserve . . ."

Don't spend another minute being one who takes a pass on bragging because of a belief that, in the grand scheme of life, what goes around will come around. In time, you will be noticed and acclaimed. Not always, not even very often . . . possibly never.

You can be your own worst enemy or your own best friend. Get your name in the yellow pages of life—advertise your good efforts and accomplishments. Something could miss you completely that should have been yours—it could happen. It's not fair. Real but not fair.

Here's a phrase I've used when talking about the neces-

sity to take credit for your accomplishments. When someone compliments you on **anything**, respond with these six
magic words.

Thank you for recognizing my magnificence.

Now, you may think this sounds a tad outrageous, even
ridiculous. My audiences laugh and think it's a hoot when
I tell them this. But it works.

Life isn't going to be fair all of time. If you truly want
your share of the pie, it's essential to speak up and speak
out. Take credit for the great (and the small but wonderful) things you do. And, yes, just getting out of bed in the
morning counts.

JB's Keeper #11
***Life—it's sometimes too long, too hard, and
not fair. Have one anyway.***

Chapter Ten

 Negative Self-Talk—
You Aren't Wrong

A few years ago, I was invited to speak at a conference in Billings, Montana. More than 500 men and women in the community were expected. After details were worked out and contracts signed, I received a call from one of the program chairs five months before the event. She invited me to play in a Celebrity Golf Tournament to be held while I was in Montana. I said, "Sure, I would love to play in the event. What did I need to do?"

She asked if I played golf. I said, "No. But with five months to learn, surely I would have the fundamentals down to a tee!" When I told my husband John that I had just agreed to play in a golf tournament at the end of summer, his face registered disbelief. "Judith, you don't have a clue what you are getting into. You need to practice every day."

"Huh?" was my response. "I don't have the time to

practice everyday. It doesn't look that complicated. After all, we did follow Jack Nicklaus around the golf course in Pebble Beach several years ago. What could possibly be so hard about hitting a ball with a stick into a hole in the grass?" John just shook his head and smiled at me.

At about the same time, he had renewed his interest in golf—his choice of recreation. He was thrilled to have a golf partner under the same roof. He also had two other partners down the street; our friends Pete and Robin were willing comrades on the links. Pete, the supreme master of the foursome, constantly reminded us with his expertise how incredibly amateurish we three were.

The maximum handicap allowed in golf is 40. If the average par for a course is 72, a person (yours truly included) can, with this 40-stroke handicap, score 112 and have a good day. "Nothing to it," I proclaimed. Sports have always come easy for me; 112 strokes for eighteen holes— no problem. Reduce the score by 40 and I'd be shooting what the big boys shot! This would be as easy as one, two, and three.

Wrong, wrong, wrong. In my early efforts, I wasn't able to hit 112 on a good day—try 140 to 150 instead. But my scores weren't nearly as bad as the transition in my vocabulary. It was unbelievable how angry I would get with myself. "What's wrong with me? I'm so stupid . . . a jerk . . . a disaster . . . a failure." And those were the light rebukes. When I really got ticked, the mental and verbal assault of myself was quite awesome.

How could this supposedly non-violent game make me feel so violent? When others heard I had taken up the "sticks," I could always count on a comment or two. So, feeling quite defensive about my efforts to learn the game, I'd commonly fire back with, "You know why they call it golf? Because all the other four-letter words were taken."

Needless to say, I wasn't a happy camper. How could this be called a game—it surely wasn't any fun, at least for me. I underestimated the dedication of time and effort that playing the game of golf required. It took me almost two years to get myself back in balance and to stop verbally beating myself up. During those two years, I was a "jerk" to be around. I couldn't stand myself on the golf course. Neither could my friends and husband. Bummer!

The more negative and angry I felt, the worse I played. I expected to have a bad day even before I even hit the first ball! A self-fulfilling prophecy—a bad habit. Finally, I said enough—this stress and anger "t'aint" good. The barrage of negative self-talk was beginning to impact everyone and everything around me.

I'm Just A Mom ...

Louise is a documentation specialist for an international shipping line. She has been in the paid work force for only a few short years, and wears two hats—she's a mother of five children, too. She works with several managers who are younger and have fewer family responsibilities than she has. Her negative self-talk tells her that they, because of their age, experience, and freedom from responsibility, are better than she is. In her words,

> I feel that I'm in an awkward spot. Several managers are younger than me and have more experience in the business world. I feel that my life experiences should make me more capable than they are, but I'm in a much lower position.
>
> I'm scared to go for a management position, even though I'm capable of it. I keep telling myself I am just a mom, and moms don't make good business managers.

Raising five children and working outside the home involves a lot of well-honed management skills. Granted, it is a stretch to envision that a mother of five is a qualified "business manager." But what's required is only a few stepping stones away, so—why not? The real problem is Louise's negative self-talk. What she has internalized is probably evident at work. Her first step is to reverse the "I can't," to "I can."

Mixed Signals

Sue recalls that her mother worked outside the home when she was growing up, but was always home when Sue returned from school. Her mother did volunteer work around her children's schedules. Then, as Sue's high school graduation neared, she sensed the general expectation that young women should go to college, and not just for the MRS degree. She realized she was getting mixed messages:

> My parents never said I should go to college but I expected it for myself, and I graduated with a degree in education. My mother did volunteer work, and never was in the paid work force. It's great to have a mom at home; on the other hand, it's important to be an accomplished person who can get things done in the workplace. I felt pulled from both sides.
>
> If I chose to be a homemaker, that was fine with some and not with others. And if I decided to work outside the home, that would be fine with some and not with others. I would end up with self-doubts, not knowing which voice to listen to.

After much indecision and struggle, Sue now spends her time volunteering in her community with emphasis in helping the local hospital. She has made her family her primary career and professional volunteerism her outside interest. Finally happy with her chosen path, she has learned to neutralize the criticism she received from others—and overcome mixed messages she had been internalizing as self-doubt.

There Will Always Be Naysayers

Mark works in the senior management of a company that employs 500 men and women. He also is one of the principals who redesigned how their workplace was organized. When the reorganization plan was put in place, grumbling started and Mark found the criticism hard to take, as he explained:

> I received a lot of flak and criticism once the restructuring was done. Comments included statements like: the entire reorganization plan was stupid; we were going into areas we had no business being in; the business would shut down and we would all be bounced out. I took all the criticism personally; I began to feel paranoid and even doubted my self-worth.

When criticism lands in your lap as it did with Mark, it is common to be sensitized by it. Change makes people uncomfortable—some even fearful—so they grumble. Realize that naysayers are the inevitable product of change. They direct their frustrations toward the person they believe to be responsible for their discomfort. In this case, it was Mark. Because of the criticism, he plunged into self-doubt, a form of self-sabotage that led to questioning his own skills and recommendations.

Negative Self-Talk

Any type of negative self-talk, from "I'm a jerk for blowing the presentation" to "I'm worthless and shouldn't be alive," is destructive and paralyzing. When your inner voice says your idea, your concept, your work, your friendship (whatever) is useless and has no value, you come down with a paralytic virus. That virus infects your thought processes so completely that you progressively believe all your ideas and efforts are a waste of your time and everybody else's.

Remember Shirley Davalos in Chapter 2? She sabotaged her chances of getting the job she wanted to with negative self-talk. Davalos took it a step further by verbalizing her doubts. She did not believe she could fill the position and she said so—to the decision-maker, the person who wanted to hire her. Her self-talk stalled her career for five years.

I believed I would never be able to hit a golf ball straight—much less into a little hole in the grass. I needed an attitude lobotomy to get back on the right track. First, I had to be very realistic with the amount of time available for recreational activities and how much of that time would be spent on the game of golf. I didn't have lots.

I told my husband I would probably never be a good golfer; I just couldn't commit to the needed hours of practice that he could. We both needed to lower our expectations of what I could and could not do. After that, I stopped keeping score because it drove me nuts comparing how I did with others in the foursome. Most importantly, I released myself from the need to play "perfectly." I backed away from my competitive spirit, knowing that if I didn't, the negative self-talk demons would take control again.

When you fill your mind with statements like "I am too young, I am too old, I don't have the talent, I didn't go

to college, I can't use the computer, I can't type, I can't
_____ , I'm not _____ , I don't have _____ ," you lose. You
are infected with the negative self-talk virus. Your inner
voice gradually paralyzes you and takes you down further
and further with each variation of the "I can'ts."

Steps to Positive Self-Talk

The following steps will get you off the negative self-talk
track.

1. *Be objective in evaluating why the negative self-talk*
   surfaces.

   Is the criticism valid? Is this the most important
   issue in your life? Put things into perspective, as I
   did with golf. If I couldn't make the time to
   practice, why in the world should I beat myself up
   for not getting better? Berating myself was an
   unrealistic consequence of my golf score. And, I
   told hubby to knock it off—stop asking me how
   many "ruined shots" did I have!

2. *Identify "what is" and "what is not" realistic in*
   your words of negative self-talk.

   Are people giving you mixed messages? The goals
   of others need not be yours; you don't have to be
   good at everything—just good at what is important.
   Define what is really important in your life. I
   asked myself if my golfing ability (or lack of it)
   would impact my success in my work or my sense
   of who I really am. The answer was a definite,
   NO! My expectations had been unrealistic. My new
   attitude became "who cares—do what you can with

your skill, and when you can, improve them."
Now, it's no big deal whether I get a par or a
quadruple bogey!

3. Determine what you are afraid of.

Most negative self-talk arises when a fear button is
pushed. Would I look stupid if I swung and missed
the ball on the tee? (Yes, but good players do, too).
Would I appear incompetent if I dribbled the ball
only a few feet off the tee? (See answer above).
Would I look like a total failure if shot after shot to
the green missed by several feet each time? (See
above. And, yes, I'm quite good at this one). Here's
the bottom line—if I blow the shot, does my life or
do people I care for depend on my doing it
perfectly right? No, No and more Noes.

4. Substitute positive self-talk.

Ah, sometimes it's easier said than done. But
definitely possible. Find one good thing, make a
mental tape of what worked, then replay it.
Replace the negative with something new. It could
include taking a class, reading a book,
brainstorming with a trusted friend, even seeing a
movie. The movie *Tin Cup* starring Kevin Costner
made my day and definitely helped bring my golf
expectations into balance. Costner's character blew
it, but he had a great ride along the way.

5. Create a list of affirmative sentences that are meaningful to you—not someone else.

Frequent reminders to change your negative self-
talk can make a big difference. Put each of them

on a 3 x 5 card and review them frequently throughout the day. I know many who tape these cards to mirrors all over their house and in their car. Post-its or sticky pads work great too.

Consider these sample sentences to get you started:

> *I am a loving wife and mother . . .*
> *I am a terrific father and husband . . .*
> *I am an incredible worker . . .*
> *I am alive and well and healthy . . .*
> *I am at peace with the world . . .*
> *I am fun to be around.*
> *I am . . . etc., etc., etc.*

JB's Keeper #12
When you substitute positive self-talk
for negative self-talk—
and reinforce the change by telling others—
you will increase your self-esteem
and self-confidence.

As with other behaviors involving self-sabotage, feedback from an outside source is invaluable to get you off the negative self-talk track. With your new outlook, the sky becomes your new limit. A true win-win.

Chapter Eleven

 Mind Reading—
A Skill to Develop

For years, my family has watched Star Trek, from the original series through the latest Star Trek offspring—Voyager. One of the series' most popular characters is Counselor Troi who has unique qualities. She's able to sense, feel and, at times, read others' minds. She can communicate with others of her race without saying a word.

Do you expect others to read your mind and anticipate your needs, your wants, or desires? In books about the differences between men and women, we commonly find that both make assumptions about the other. I regard this as a form of mind reading.

You probably feel your spouse or significant other should instinctively *know* what you need or want in a specific situation without you giving specifics about your desires. This is another form of mind reading that can be very practical . . . and can be learned.

Learning To Project

To learn to anticipate what someone else needs or wants from you, start by putting into perspective everything you know about this person—current status and past. When you know what makes him or her tick, you have a much better chance of projecting what may come next. Develop this skill of projecting and others will think you can read minds.

Whenever you display what looks like, even feels like, mind reading, you are really observing the direct result of your own learning behavior. As the bell curve below shows, 20 percent of the general population is incredibly observant. They are above average, even superior, in their ability to anticipate what others need. That ability has been derived from their pattern of observing others with both their needs and wants in mind.

Observational (Mind Reading) Learning

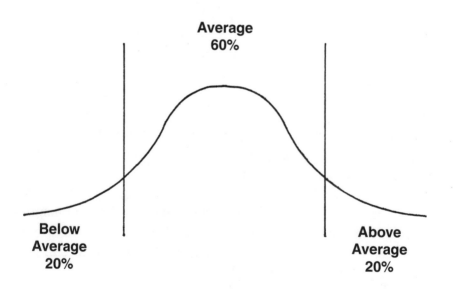

Average
60%

Below
Average
20%

Above
Average
20%

Another 20 percent of the general population is on the other end of the curve. They are below average in their ability to observe and, therefore, below average in anticipating the needs and wants of another.

The phrase of the '90s "he doesn't get it, she doesn't get it, they don't get it" is appropriate when evaluating this bell curve. The 20 percent below average group doesn't get it. In short, clueless. The 60 percent mid-section group—the bulk of the population—will perhaps get it if given a little bit more time. Since the majority has average observation skills, those who are above average—possibly you—might experience a high degree of frustration, even anger.

If you are above average, you are most likely independent, self-directed and need minimal, if any, checking up on. You are in control, self-reliant and self-confident. If you have a job, managers or supervisors are most likely to point you out as the "model." They may get irritated when they can't figure out why the rest of the team can't work with the same initiative as you do. Their attitude/assumption—a form of mind reading—leads them to conclude that the same qualities and traits you demonstrate should be consistent throughout the organization.

Let's look on the other side of the coin (and I think it's appropriate for me to plead guilty here). I like conversation to move fairly quickly and sometimes I jump the gun. It comes as no surprise to family and friends when I finish a sentence for them. This happens because I know the person so well; I just have a feel for where they are going. Or if I am watching television or a movie, I commonly come up with the next lines before the actors say them.

I concede that this can bother people and sometimes gets me in trouble. Because my mind speeds along so quickly, I expect everyone else to be on the same train running at the same speed I am. When I look back—which I confess is not frequently—and discover they have taken a few detours, I'm annoyed, mostly at myself.

For the person good at mind reading, being impatient is a common trait. It reminds me of when I was in grade school. All my report cards often had comments on them—about talking too much, interrupting, and passing notes (little did I know that note-writing would lead to writing books and talking too much to becoming a speaker). My teachers also noted that I was too impatient. People who do not keep up at the same pace can become irritants. But they will get to the point eventually. A little patience might be in order.

Is Mind Reading Important?

In a word, yes. It only takes a little bit to be above average, to transition from the majority of the population into the above-average minority of the population. Why? Because mind reading, or at least a form of it, is a survival skill. My experience has been that women often think others (men) can read their minds, and should really tell them how good they are. That way, they don't need to boast or brag. Why should they be forced to openly take credit for a project, a concept, or idea they created and delivered? They incorrectly assume that everyone knows what a great job they have done.

Aggressive reorganization of companies and enterprises has occurred frequently in the past few years, so employees who were mum about their accomplishments and credits were often let go. They felt stunned when they received a "pink slip." They couldn't believe their value and those who made the layoff decisions did not know the quality of their work. They assumed the decision-makers could mind read. And their assumption was wrong.

With a little mind reading of their own, they should have figured out that the decisions weren't made psychically.

Tools for Your Survival Kit

When managers within an organization see you in that upper 20 percent (above average in skills and learning), you are on the inside track. That's also true when committee leaders recognize your ability to size up a situation quickly. They both value your input and opinions. You may be their next trailblazer—they want you.

To help you transition into the above-average club, these tools added to your survival kit will also enhance your mind-reading skills.

✓ *Sharpen your sense of humor.*
   Few like to work or play with people who are sour-pusses or take themselves too seriously. Be able to laugh at yourself. It encourages others to view you as OK and opens the channels for knowing them. Mind reading follows easily.
✓ *Be open to suggestions and criticisms*
   Sure, taking in criticisms may put you on the offensive and tick you off. But, is there a grain of truth in them? Use them as another channel of learning and connecting with others.
✓ *Give suggestions effectively and constructively.*
   A little finesse goes a long way in building relationship bridges. After evaluating a situation, offer suggestions for change, if appropriate. It's important to determine if you are in the right place and time before giving them, but those on the receiving end will see you as an ally and will understand their situation better.

✓ **Be observant.**

How do others in positions above you act, behave, and even dress? Are there events, happenings or causes that superiors in your organization sponsor? Those who have transitioned from being a staff employee to an administrator or manager have learned to observe two sides to any situation, sometimes more. Try on the shoes you think you want to wear. That also helps you anticipate what's going on for others.

✓ **Attitude counts always.**

You may be an extremely talented person, but if your attitude is sulky, moody, and abrasive—you name it—who wants to be with you? Your bad attitude gets in the way of getting to know others well, so you weaken your ability to anticipate others' actions and thoughts.

✓ **Show up.**

This seems to be a logical and common-sense point, but too often tardiness, cutting a day short, even using sick days as goof-off times can be a lost opportunity for sharpening your observation skills, and getting to know people.

Kit was a manager in a communications department at a life insurance company. While his staff took responsibility of various ongoing assignments, Kit saw his role as gathering "big picture" information that would influence these staff and affect the organization. He served on high-level committees and networked with key managers in every department of the company. His activities helped him anticipate the changes and prepare his staff in their community's roles. Some would call Kit a mind reader because he always seemed to be "in the know." In reality, he put all these skills to work and made a lot of friends in the process.

Develop Your Communication Skills

If you run into a brick wall because you have assumed incorrectly that another knows what you want, take some steps to improve your communication skills.

✓ *Never assume anything.*

It may be as clear as a bell to you, but others may not share the clarity of your viewpoint. And, though this issue may be a priority to you, they likely need convincing to move it up on their list.

✓ *Talk to the right people in a precise way.*

With time economy in mind, communicate your need or want *only* to someone who can make it happen. Tailor your spiel to the intended recipient, using language that is precise, to the point and clearly understandable. This requires an awareness of the inherent differences in culture/race, gender, age, upbringing, religious preference, etc. Take time to get to know the person(s) you are going to talk to.

✓ *Listen.*

Listening is paramount. It takes time to develop *effective* listening skills. Set the stage, when possible, so as to keep distractions to a minimum and don't allow others to interrupt. Make sure you appear attentive to what is being said—don't doodle or display boredom with careless body language.

✓ *Praise with sincerity.*

Praise helps build lines of communication but is only as good as the sincerity behind it. It doesn't work, and could work against you, if the person receiving your praise feels it's insincere or artificial.

Realize that punishing for negative behavior is less effective than rewarding positive actions. People *do* remember praise and will seek it out.

What is mind reading all about, really? In simple words, it is your overall ability to interpret the actions, then anticipate the needs of an individual or a group. Does mind reading have anything to do with ESP or psychic skills? Maybe. For most of us, it's a learned skill that has great value in all facets of our lives. Some call it intuition.

No matter what camp you are in—that of the naturally gifted or the skilled learner—never take anything for granted. Be alert, avoid complacency, and develop your own strategy for assimilating the messages around you. With practice you can avoid many self-sabotaging behaviors and bad scenarios. And, as a mind reader, you can foresee and thus direct the outcome of many circumstances.

> *JB's Keeper #13*
> *Anyone can be a mind reader;*
> *you need to keep your eyes and ears open*
> *and withhold judgements.*

Chapter Twelve

The Abuse-Excuse Chain— Don't Get Caught In It

Bad news, elections, and celebrities usually fill the medias space—it doesn't matter if it's radio, TV, print or the Internet. News—whether it's good or bad (and usually the bad stuff gets top billing), we hear about it. Who will forget President Bill Clinton's fiasco with intern Monica Lewinsky? How about President George W. Bush's late hour revelation of a DUI or all those chads in Florida? What about the Challenger explosion? The murder of Jon Bonet Ramsey? The Exxon Valdez oil mess? Robert Downey Jr's. drug arrests? The incredible mishandling of Dr. Lee at the Los Alamos Lab in New Mexico? Or the U.S. Submarine and Japanese fishing boat mishap in Hawaii? Then there's Waco, Supreme Court Justice Clarence Thomas' confirmation hearing, the Oklahoma City bombing and Jesse Jackson's love child. Bad news, elections and celebrities.

Problems. Problems. Problems. With every problem,

especially a public one, there are a group of individuals dedicated to changing the wind—creating a more favorable (hopefully) environment for their clients. They are called "spin-doctors." Men and women who make their living by changing, twisting and sometimes distorting the problem for the benefit of their clients via the media. Truth has little to do with it.

Spin-doctors. They are the masters of rationale. They explain and literally make excuses for why things did or didn't happen as planned. Businesses also have spin-doctors known as public relations specialists. The political species are far and away the most prolific purveyors of "double-speak." Their "spin" on the indiscretions of candidates can be as ridiculous as "the devil made me do it."

Spin-doctors think incredibly fast on their feet. It's their gift! Their silver tongues deliver a barrage of words in such a torrent that, at times, you wonder if they know what they're talking about. But they are good at what they do; they are articulate and sound intelligent. Surely they must be credible. At least, that's what their clients want the public to think. It's smart to always remember that spin-doctors and PR firms are paid by the person or group who has the problem. What they you—the public—hear is not necessarily the truth.

There's also the pseudo spin-doctors—all those journalists and columnists who write about what ever their passions are, including yours truly. I have opinions. I write columns for several publications. I'm on TV and radio quite a bit. My opinions are mine—and I share them, trying to influence others to my way of thinking.

Now let's look in the mirror, I'll bet you've tried your hand at spin-doctoring. You may have come up with rationalizations and excuses that have been pretty lame. Which of these sound familiar? "I was too busy" or "I'll do it later" or "I've had a bad day" or "I deserve this" or "I'm sorry" or "I didn't mean to" or "I forgot." I suspect that you have a few more "old reliables" up your sleeve. Some people turn excuse making into an art form. They may not know it, but they are spin-doctors too.

Whether used in business, personal or political scenarios, the spin-doctor routine is the ultimate in making excuses. With well-executed spin doctoring, a negative situation can be made to appear positive. This type of rationale in the case of an unjustifiable termination could be: "Sloan is such a talented hard working person, he just needed a kick in the pants to make him use his abilities." At home, a spin-doctored statement from a procrastinator might be: "The dinner wasn't ready on time because I wanted it to be piping hot when you got home." The most talented excuse makers can fool some of the people some of the time, but rarely all the time. It's easier to deceive yourself than others when you habitually proffer excuses.

What's Good About Excuses?

If excuses are so bad, what could possibly be good about them? An excuse can offer relief from the internal turmoil of something done incorrectly. Relief comes because you don't have to deal with the situation now; it can wait. If the excuse really works, it will relieve tension that can create negativity and give you time to think things out calmly. If you face the loss of business, fatal damage to a relationship, or even getting fired, an excuse may give you the time needed to achieve a more favorable outcome.

Many people use excuses and deny events in order to escape. In tense situations, rarely is anyone at peak performance, let alone acting graciously. Instead, people act out, shout, and say things they wish they never had. So a good excuse allows for a temporary escape from the tension.

Though people may know an excuse is plain baloney, most want to believe it. Why? It creates fewer hassles. You often hear a justification like: "It doesn't impact me directly, so what does it matter?"

Maureen first went to work in the retail industry after her youngest child went to college. Before that, she spent a lot of time doing community work—serving on committees, volunteering at both the kids' schools and her church. Because her mother had died of stomach cancer, she also volunteered at her local hospital for events designed to increase public awareness of cancer.

All this sounds great, but Maureen had a secret and she covered it up quite well. Maureen was a drinker. During the afternoon hours she would often meet her girlfriends for several glasses of wine. She was always home before her family began arriving for dinner, so they didn't seem to suspect anything. When her kids went off to college, she found more empty time in her day. Her husband worked late, so an afternoon drink sometimes led to the downing of an entire bottle. Alcohol wasn't the problem, she rationalized. She just needed to be busier, so she would get a job. Here's Maureen's story,

> I always liked to work with people, so when my daughter went off to college, I decided to get a job I would get paid for. I always liked shopping so it seemed ideal to work in a retail store that had lots of customer contact. With my volunteer background, I landed a job in customer service.
>
> Initially, I loved it. But I found myself dealing a lot with customers' excuses for why they didn't pay their bill or why they were returning items. After a while, I tired of the excuses. And found myself taking longer and longer lunches.

At lunch, I would order my customary glass of wine. As the routine of the job set in, my boredom level increased. And, as customers became more irritable with our company's return policy, I rationalized why I should have an extra glass of wine. I would tell myself, "You really took a lot of garbage from that customer. You deserve one." Or even, "This job is so stressful with the amount of verbal abuse I take every day, I need it."

Then I started to get into trouble. I would return late from lunch; sometimes I didn't go back at all. Or I would cut my afternoon short and head off to have cocktails with my girlfriends. A few times I called in sick, or just came in late. I thought I was pretty clever and could cover for my absences, but I was wrong. My supervisor as well as others in the department started to complain. When I was confronted, I denied everything. Being late, taking off early, and snapping at customers—you name it—it was on my excuse list.

The best thing that happened was my supervisor confronting me. She referred me to the company's employees assistance program (EAP). I told her I didn't need any assistance. Her counter was, "If you want to work here, you do." I made the appointment and learned the program assists employees with problems that interfered with their productivity. I wasn't the only one; I found that others sought help with gambling, money problems, domestic violence, smoking and, yes, drinking.

It wasn't easy but I signed up and began counseling. The company paid for all of it. I recognized I had used my drinking problem not only as a crutch but also as a brace to prop me up because

of my mother's death, the aloneness I felt after
the kids left, and my husband's involvement
with his career. Today, I'm happy and I feel in
control. I also feel some anger toward myself for
denying for so long that I had a problem and
depended on alcohol.

Maureen is just one of millions who suffer from substance abuse. And for all of them, denial of the abuse is the
rule, not the exception—"Not me, I don't have a problem."
Many companies like Maureen's push for sobriety, though
they have leaner structures these days and can't afford the
luxury of "carrying" the substance abuser. Identifying employees with problems can be especially difficult for companies that employ telecommuters (they work out of their
homes) or offer flex time to workers (where the employee
doesn't have a full shift contact with managers).

Companies have also learned that employees with substance abuse problems are three to four times more likely to have accidents on the job, and five times more likely
to file a workmen's compensation claim. The financial
drain that results from both is substantial.

Few can overcome substance abuse by themselves.
But no program will work unless you first recognize the
problem and make a commitment to change it.

If Not Now, Then Later

Eventually an excuse catches up with you. The primary
purpose for using them in the first place is to delay an
event or consequence to a future time. In some cases, the
matter will be forgotten altogether. But here's the problem. If you don't face issues as they present themselves,
you may lose out on the opportunity to learn from them.

The news in the media is always chock full of events that started off very small and grew into major mountains. Think about some of the financial fiascoes in the past years. One that comes to mind involves a young trader who managed various investment accounts for his employer, a British bank. He started trading on his own, had some wins and some losses. Initially, the wins exceeded the losses.

His first successes that lured him eventually hooked him. He began to trade more and more and soon the wins turned into losses of great magnitude. Adept at paper shuffling, he was able to hide his losses for many months. Eventually he could no longer manipulate the facts to cover the severity of the losses.

The end result? The bank went under—billions of dollars lost. The employee? He's in jail. Because his reports were timely, his supervisors rarely scrutinized their content. If they did, he would employ his mastery of the plausible excuse. His supervisors were lulled by the simple fact that he was making the company a lot of money. But his cover-ups were eventually inadequate to hide the mountain of losses his trading improprieties had incurred. They led to his and his employer's downfall.

Excuses Are Everywhere

Most work places and relationships have a certain level of tolerance for excuses. It seems that each of us has a type of internal tally system for each person we contact. When the tally sheet gets filled up, relationships and even jobs can be in jeopardy. If you are the guilty one, your credibility takes a dive. And once you lose credibility, few care about what you feel, say, or even do. You've blown it.

Sometimes excuses challenge the integrity of another. These challenges could be statements like:

You made me do it.

He's always picking on me.

At least my error wasn't as bad as yours.

If you had only listened to me, you wouldn't have made the mistake.

I wouldn't have made the mistake if you hadn't given me the wrong information.

And, though not a challenge of one's integrity, people use this popular techno-excuse:

The computer is down; I can't get the information.

A malfunctioning computer system can be legitimate, but some use this excuse automatically. Because of our dependence on these machines, the computer excuse is among the most irritating.

Ridding Our Lives of Excuses

Let's not confuse excuses with explanations, which are a factual review of something in the past. Instead of using an excuse, find out what's really going on and turn an excuse into a truthful explanation. Proper use of an explanation allows the parties to evaluate the situation and develop a strategy to correct it. While explanations are good, take care not to let an excuse creep into the dialog. An explanation could be: "I'm sorry, I didn't understand you needed the report by this date. My intention is to still help you. What would you like me to do now?" Another could be: "I'm sorry, I made a mistake. Here's what I'll do to fix it."

From that point on, anger is diffused and common sense begins to surface. Though damage may have been done, it's been neutralized and hopefully allows you to move forward.

Take a point from one of my favorite department stores, Nordstrom. Management there doesn't tolerate excuses. Nordstrom has just has one written rule for all employees. It's this: "In your best judgment, do whatever you can to satisfy the customer. Don't offer excuses. Deal with the problem and fix it." Sounds like a good way to do business. Unfortunately, most merchants don't have that philosophy . . . nor do most individuals.

Confronting the Excuse Head-on

To financially support my family, I write books and speak to audiences around the country. Speaking means traveling, which puts me in a lot of airports. I live in Colorado so I find myself frequently at Denver International Airport— DIA as we call it.

On the road, I take care of speaking and my husband John handles selling books and tapes. Because airport security has increased over the past few years, we have befriended some of the skycaps who know our routine and make our check-in easier. And let's face it, it's more pleasant when a friend greets you along the way. Tony has become our most regular guy at check-in.

On one trip to Philadelphia, we drove along DIA's curbside, opened the doors, and began to unload five 50-pound boxes of books plus our suitcase to check them in. When I pulled out my traveling wallet to reach for the tickets, they were missing. I panicked. A return home to look for them would take a minimum of an hour and half under the best of circumstances.

Going back wasn't an option because our flight would be leaving in 50 minutes. In desperation I turned to Tony and said, "Help, I can't find my tickets, what should I do?" His response was: "Find them," then he added, "or buy two more tickets and get a refund for the lost ones when you find them." No way did I want to buy more tickets. Coach tickets would cost a minimum of $1200 each—the lost ones cost 50 percent less because they were purchased well in advance of our trip. I said, "That won't work. What else could I do?"

"Find them," was Tony's response again. He offered to go through my ticket wallet, the one used exclusively for travel-related items. With determination, I declared I would look one more time. As I dumped everything out, low and behold, I found my tickets.

When Tony said, "Find them or buy new ones," I knew those were the only options. I didn't like the latter, so I had to put more energy into the former. To overcome any tendency to make excuses, consider handling them as firmly as Tony handled me: confront, give the options, and then get on with it.

If you have found yourself in a situation when you said, "I'm too busy" or "I forgot" or "The computer is down" or "_____," stop to curb your excuse making. And if that curbing can't come from you, it might have come from someone else who has the backbone to say something like this—

> "I'm sorry you are busy, but those reports were due in today. Have them on my desk by 4 PM or else." In the case of the computer, "I know computers do great things but where is your back-up? Don't you keep it on another disk? Find a way to access it and have those on my desk by 4 o'clock."

Take heed, you've been caught in an excuse.

If a supervisor, co-worker or friend confronts you about an excuse and doesn't offer a consequence (i.e., suspension, job at risk, withdrawal of friendship), there's little to make you want to alter your behavior. Your excuse worked! But when there's a consequence and possible negative outcome, you are most likely to heed the warnings. And when others hand you a pile of excuses, communicate consequences to them as appropriate. Doing so is more likely to help build relationships than destroy them.

What's Your Excuse Quotient?

Take this quiz to see if you are an excuse abuser by answering *Never, Seldom, Sometimes,* or *Often* to these questions:

_____ Do you usually think it's someone else's fault or problem when you don't complete a task on time?

_____ Do you ever attribute your problems to someone else's performance?

_____ Do you ever attribute your problems to plain old bad luck?

_____ When things are not going well, are you likely to say, "I'm just having a bad day"?

_____ Do you think your managers or family members put unrealistic expectations on you?

_____ Do you ever rationalize why things don't get done?

_____ When you are having a bad day, do you usually wish you worked in another place?

_____ When you don't complete a task, do you ever respond, "I'm too busy"?

_____ Have you put something off with the statement, "I'll do it later"?

_____ Have you rationalized not completing a task with the statement, "I forgot"?

If you answered *Often* to five or six of the questions, you may place too much emphasis and blame on outside factors instead of on yourself. Though sometimes excuses work, as a rule they don't. They eventually catch up with you.

How can you alter the excuse-abuse chain? These five steps will help you overcome your habits of self-sabotaging excuse making.

1. *Be accountable.*

Good intentions are always terrific but it's the end results that count. Evaluate yourself on the results of your actions.

2. *Evaluate your dialogue.*

How do you sound to others? Pay close attention to what you tell yourself. If you do, your "aware self" will not let you get away with excuse making— internally or externally.

3. *Step back.*

Pretend you are in the back of the room observing your actions and behavior. What would be your interpretation? What would your Mother see or say? See yourself as others see you.

4. *Get feedback.*

The expression "you can't see the forest for the trees" fits here. Sometimes you might be so self-involved, it's impossible to step back and observe. Ask someone to be your eyes and ears, and then listen carefully to what is said.

5. Acknowledge your progress.

Few bad habits can be changed overnight. Give yourself credit and applause with each step you make as you aim to break the abuse-excuse chain. When you come up with an excuse-free week, it's time to celebrate. Bravo!

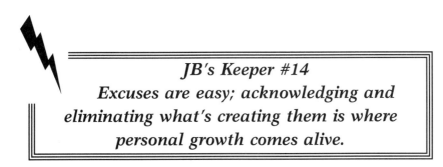

JB's Keeper #14
Excuses are easy; acknowledging and eliminating what's creating them is where personal growth comes alive.

Chapter Thirteen

 Responsibility—
Stop The Blame Game

"Victimism" is in. It's a great way to lose your job, decrease or destroy your self-esteem, and have friends and co-workers put you on their "don't call me, I'll call you" list. Are some people victims due to factors out of their control? Of course! Many, though, are victims of their own self-talk, self-attitude, and behavior. In other words, victimism is their choice.

The year 2000 was a mess for the airlines, particularly United Airlines. As both a top flyer, known as a 1K and a million mile flyer with them, I was appalled at a huge corporation's total lack of accountability and responsibility. The pilots did the Pilot Game—let's not show up so flights are cancelled (it didn't matter if passengers didn't get where they were supposed to be) so we can get more money; followed by the Mechanics Game (the flight can't go off, there might be cockroaches in the cabin, we need to check it out).

Management blamed all delays on the weather (granted the weather wasn't great, but not 100% of the time) and stonewalled customers and the media. For the first time in 25 years of speaking, I missed an engagement—and for which I originally left my home base 24 hours before the speech. It took me 26 hours to get to what was normally a three-hour flight and that included a connection. Months later, form letters were sent out with all kinds of excuses, initially even denying that there were problems with the pilots. United's customer service was the pits. For my fall schedule, I booked 24 flights with competitor Continental— we got there on time, weather problems and all!

The Victim Trap

Just how far has victimism gone? Just spend a couple of days watching the menu of problems on the talk shows. A few years ago, I did a keynote address for a community program in Wisconsin. Prior to my presentation, the local television crew came to the venue to interview me. While the technician put on my microphone, the reporter asked if I had seen the popular TV talk show *Oprah* the day before. I said no, I was en route to this event.

He went on to describe the program. Several adult children blamed their parents for their lack of confidence. He suggested I should have been on the show as a guest since I had written a book on the topic. Then he asked what I would have said to Oprah's guests of the day. I replied that, if they hadn't been battered, abused or molested by their parents, I would tell them, "Get off your rear-end, stop being victims, stop blaming everybody and take responsibility for your own actions."

Shucking off responsibility—blaming others for your actions or claiming victim status—has become the battle cry for too many people. When tennis star Jennifer Capriati was arrested for marijuana possession in the 90s, her father stepped forward and took responsibility for her actions, saying, "I pushed her too hard to compete when she was young." Maybe he did. But Jennifer is no longer a child; she's an adult. As adults, we have the ability and responsibility to step back, look in the mirror, and say, "I made the choice. . . ."

Daily, the media presents stories depicting people who claim they are not responsible for their actions. Who are these people? Some are wealthy and have privileged backgrounds, some are poverty stricken, some come from broken homes or dysfunctional families, and, last but not least, some are addicted to drugs or alcohol. They all claim to be blameless victims of whatever. But if they are not responsible for their actions/behaviors, who is?

In the old days—ten years ago—if you squandered your money on yourself for shoes, clothing, jewelry, or even drugs while neglecting to provide food for your children, society would have called you irresponsible, a misfit, and unsuitable as a parent. Today, you're excused—there must be some other reason for your actions and neglect.

A spin-off of the "psychobabble" is the redefinition of bad behavior—many now consider it a disease. The seven deadly sins are today interpreted to be behavioral complexes that are somebody else's fault!

The Honoree Flunks Out

Self-defeat and self-destruction are the twin offspring of self-sabotage; their middle name is victim. Victimism is a handicap—a barrier to your personal and professional success—and can appear at any age. The earlier it starts, the more habit forming it becomes. Take the son of a close friend, for example.

After graduating from high school at the top of his class in 1997, Jeff was invited to attend a highly sought-after engineering program at the coveted M.I.T. East Coast university. Shortly after classes started, he began to come home over the weekends. Both my friend and her husband liked that he wanted to stay in contact. After all, the campus was only two hours away and they enjoyed his stories of college life.

The family was happy until Jeff's grades were published. The university put him on academic probation; eventually he was asked not to return. The reason: straight Fs.

My friend blamed it on the educational system in New Jersey. There was nothing wrong with her son; it was someone else's fault. He then enrolled at the local community college. His next grades were a tad better: Ds. But they were certainly nothing to shout about. My friend has changed her tune. Maybe, just maybe, her son wasn't studying.

These parents allowed Jeff—even encouraged him—to come home every weekend when he first started his college career. Why? Because they sympathized with his complaints about the size of classes, the poor quality of food, the terrible dorm rooms which didn't allow him to study, etc., etc. He claimed these factors were responsible for his horrendous performance. In reality, coming home allowed him to connect with his old friends and "goof off." No homework, no studying—nothing—was done during those days. How he used his time when he was on campus was unclear.

What about his complaint that the food was "crummy"? A friend's daughter attended the same school, and reported that the food was fairly good. And if dorms are too noisy for study, there are alternatives. One is the library—one of the old-fashioned places to write papers and study texts. In truth, the newly liberated student screwed up and his parents were his silent partners.

I have no idea if this family now sees their behavior as destructive in nature. I *do* know that once an unacceptable behavior is identified, it can be altered and redirected. It certainly takes energy, effort, and perseverance.

Hear Them Whine

What about the whiners—the ones who routinely say: "Do I have to do it? Martha was late from lunch; make her do it." or "This is a crummy computer, it's always crashing." Etc., etc. Whiners love to grumble about everything; they are the first to complain and blame someone or something.

Whiners are like little kids. They do it to get attention—"look at me, listen to me." If you are the spouse, parent, or friend of a whiner, first determine if the complaint is legitimate. Then put out the clear message that whining is not allowed. When it starts up, ignore them. When it stops, acknowledge and reward them. In psychology circles, this technique is known as "behavior shaping."

For a boss or co-worker, the same advice stands. Remove yourself from the whining arena and *don't* join the gripe session. Whiners get the message when you remove yourself from earshot. Another method: when whiners are in the middle of their diatribe, ask them to give you at least two solutions—now.

From Legitimate to Illegitimate

Psychologist Caroline Zeiger is the co-author of ***Doing It All Isn't Everything***. She believes that, on the whole, the victimization notion started legitimately. There really were/are times when it was/is valid to recognize that people who are politically and physically less powerful get taken advantage of. Girls or women who are raped, people who are abused as children, even victims who get hit by a drunk driver or shot by a stray bullet can truly be called victims. Events took over their lives. Legitimate victims. Are there illegitimate ones? Yes, our court systems are filled with people grumbling about anything and everything—they make theirs and others lives miserable. These are Zeiger's ideas,

> It is important to recognize that people are taken advantage of, hurt and victimized. Nonetheless, victimization has grown to be a state of mind and a way of being in the world. This really disturbs me. It seems that people who are convinced that they are victims should sue to get what they see as their rightful due. It has become a kind of way to be in the world. In the end, it turns into a cop-out.
>
> It also puts you in a more powerless position to take the victim's posture. It says there is nothing I can do about it. The surest way to be unable to participate in solving the problem is to fail to recognize your part in creating it. There is an old cliché, "If you are not a part of the solution, then you're part of the problem." To be part of the solution, you need to recognize in what way you are part of the problem.
>
> Women are also players in this problem. They play at little girl, they play helpless, they let daddy and the troops "take care of me," as if daddy and the

troops will. A common attitude is that, "If I wait long enough for Prince Charming to come along, my life will work."

Women are usually more identified as victims than men are. They must say, "Wait a minute, if we want real equality and freedom, there are things we have to give up—like sugar daddies."

Zeiger brings up a very important point. First of all, if you don't speak up when you are faced with offensive behavior or circumstances, your silence condones it—it says it's OK. If you share jokes that could be construed as sexually oriented or suggestive, you are signaling that this is also OK. In fact, because of your participation, men could interpret that their own raunchiness is OK around this group.

The Victim Loop

Because of today's common acceptance of "it's someone else's fault," finding yourself entwined within the Victim Loop is getting too easy. Building up to victimhood follows a pattern; it is progressive but circular. It usually begins with anger or frustration, which creates a need to blame, either somebody or something. If you're the victim, you seek a target for the blame, whipping your anger into flames all the while. The target found, punishment is decided—righteous anger abounds. By the time the punishment is dealt, you've developed a full head of steam. Unfortunately, punishment rarely garners the desired results. For example, what if your target acts as if the chastening means very little to them? It starts again— the cycle continues in a continuous loop, a trap. It looks like this:

The Victim Model

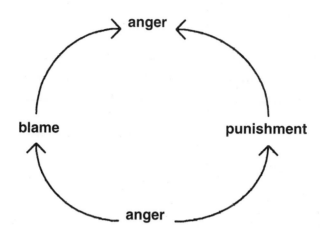

Source: The Briles Group, Inc. © 2001.

When I started playing golf a few years ago, I found myself in the Victim Loop. I got so ticked at the club, the ball, and myself (all anger creators); that I felt surely that there was a reason that I couldn't hit the damn ball (blame); that I would gear up for being ticked off even more (forward to the next anger cycle); and that I would slam the club on something—trash cans, the golf cart, bag and ground were favored targets—and practice all the four letter words that I knew (punishment). This got me absolutely nowhere. I had to clean up my act. Otherwise, no one wanted to be around me and I wouldn't/couldn't improve.

You will remain within the Victim Loop as long as you continue to blame and want to punish others. If you feel you are a victim—or others say you are acting as a victim—it is time to do a reality check. Do you like being a victim? If not, take some much needed medicine by reading on.

Break the Victim Chains

"Once a victim, always a victim" is in itself a statement that victimizes, and many believe it to be true. Being aware that you are a victim is the first step in breaking out of the loop. This awareness includes admitting you have sidestepped issues and denied responsibility, even accountability, for your part in them.

Next, identify what is making you angry. There may be several items on your list. If so, consider putting them in zones—boiling, hot, and lukewarm. Spend some quality time reviewing those in the boiling zone. You'll have time for the others later. You can't remove yourself from the jaws of the victim trap until you know why you put your foot into it in the first place.

Believe it or not, the third step is forgiveness. When you forgive, you fully release yourself from the victim mentality. Forgiveness takes a lot of heart, especially when you are a legitimate victim like the survivor of a rape or incest. Sometimes it means putting your feelings and thoughts on paper or expressed to others until you can come to grips with the anger you feel. Joining a support group may be very effective. It gives you a chance to see that your situation could be worse compared with others. And you will likely meet some role models—people who have already learned to forgive and move on. These methods help you make room for forgiveness. Remember, forgiveness does not mean you have given your approval of whatever made you angry. But it gives you relief from your pain and releases you from the agonizing feelings of victimhood.

The fourth step is to move on—forget it. Don't dredge it up again—how many times can you rehash the situation? At some point, you have to drop it if you really want

to escape from the victim trap and become psychologically healthy. You can't change history but you can change
repeating it in the future.

The final step is to take little steps. Tackle one source
of anger at a time. If new ones crop up, tell yourself, "I
won't allow myself to be pulled back. I'm not going to
blame someone else if something doesn't go my way." For
reinforcement, get a trusted friend or co-worker to help
you develop a feedback system.

Victim Free Model

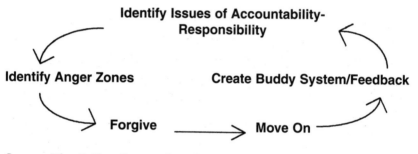

Source: The Briles Group, Inc. © 2001.

As a rule, no behavior is changed overnight. It is highly probable you will have to be reminded (reinforced)
more than once that some reactions or responses are inappropriate. It's also important to develop realistic expectations for yourself and those you share your life with. You
cannot change anyone but yourself. Don't be surprised or
disappointed if others fail to notice your progress. They
won't change their reactions to you overnight, but it
doesn't mean they can't change either. Ask yourself:

➢ How might I *change* my attitude and behavior to
   make it more difficult for others to victimize me?

> ➤ How can I *resolve* the problem?
> ➤ Will blaming someone else *change* the situation?
> ➤ If I remain a victim, does it *solve* anything?
> ➤ If I remain a victim, do I *really* feel better?
> ➤ If I remain a victim, will I *gain* respect?
> ➤ Ideally, what *should* the situation look or feel like?

If you communicate your likes and dislikes, as well as what constitutes unacceptable behavior around you, you will have begun your victimless life. You'll gradually find yourself back in the driver's seat, in charge of your own destiny. You will recognize that you *and you alone* are making the right decisions for you—not your parents, your spouse, your children, your associates, your co-workers, your boss, the government, the media, etc. etc. You are no longer a victim. And that, dear reader, is victorious.

When you deny yourself the vogue of victimism, you stop blaming others. Don't spend another day sinking further into the self-sabotage of being a victim. Believe in yourself.

JB's Keeper #15
You have the sole responsibility (and capability) for making any necessary change to delete victimitis. Forget about trying to have power over others; just work on having power over you.

Chapter Fourteen

Revenge—
Only Sweet In The Short Term

I can remember my father saying, "Hell hath no fury like a woman scorned." Later, when I was in high school, I heard fellow students saying, "Don't get mad, get even." Are these sayings you remember, too? Both have ingredients of truth.

When you don't sabotage yourself, you can take a "no" answer (scorn) in stride and will quickly find a new direction. If the scorn is criticism—deserved or undeserved— you will use it to correct a fault or tell the critic he or she is wrong, and why.

Unfortunately, too many fail to take control of a situation on a timely basis and, when they finally act, they weaken their response with anger. Anger can be the result of procrastination that grew out of frustration with their inability to take charge. You may have everyone's attention when you are in the midst of the fury of anger, but your words will be heavily discounted.

It's tempting to take the offense when someone has made you angry. But "getting even" effectively takes planning and usually puts the plotter in a negative (self-defeating) frame of mind. It could be a futile effort, too, because the person who is the focus of your anger probably has a great deal of practice fending off righteous indignation. It isn't likely you are the first one to be attacked by this person. If you must vent, a simple response could be,

"You're full of hot air. Your attack on me doesn't warrant any rebuttal. I feel certain this isn't the first time you have been told that."

Feeling angry is not an indication you are abnormal. It doesn't mean you are unstable, unbalanced, or unhealthy unless you are angry a good bit of the time. Let's face it, everyone at some time is going to get ticked off. The important thing is dealing with your anger. How you direct it will determine whether your reaction is stable or unstable, balanced or unbalanced.

When Anger Turns to Revenge

Lana is a therapist and an author. She found herself at the receiving end of a vendetta directed by another woman who initially offered her help. The help turned into a quagmire of legal threats delivered on an answering machine.

While visiting a friend in New England, Lana met Helene through a mutual friend. Lana mentioned she was working on a new book. Helene's eyes lit up—she said she was a terrific researcher and loved to write. Helene suggested she help Lana research and write the book, even offering to go to Lana's Florida home. Lana just had to provide her with a place to stay for a few days. Helene would review the material, then take it from there. To Lana, the proposal sounded ideal; she felt she worked better when she had someone with whom she could share ideas.

After some correspondence, a financial agreement was reached and Helene flew to Florida. Upon her arrival, Lana showed Helene all her personal notes, the latest abstracts on the topic, and the complete literature research she had done. Lana's collection of books and articles that covered the topic were also made accessible to Helene. Lana took time to explain ideas, philosophies, and feelings about the book while Helene made extensive notes. They then taped several hours of directions that Lana wanted. She said she would transcribe additional tapes and forward them to Helene.

After Helene returned to New England, Lana evaluated their session and came to a sobering conclusion. Helene wasn't in a position to provide the creative input Lana had first expected. Realizing this wasn't the right fit, she immediately wrote to Helene and told her so.

That's when the battle began. Helene called and demanded Lana's notes and tapes, even though earlier they had agreed Lana would have the tapes transcribed but that the notes were her personal property. Thinking about it later, she felt that Helene's attitude was inappropriate. Two days later, a Friday, she got a call from Helene's attorney who announced he was making arrangements to have the notes and tapes picked up. Lana brushed him off, saying, "You've got to be kidding." She thought that would be the end of it.

The attorney called back later that day. Lana had turned her answering machine on and was flabbergasted when she listened to his message. She explained it this way,

He said he was instructed to take action Monday morning at 10 AM if I did not give him the notes and tapes. Things would come out in litigation that would be detrimental to my professional as well as my personal life.

Early Saturday morning, Lana got another threatening call on her machine saying she would have to pay all legal fees ranging from $5,000 to $6,000 each for the tapes and the notes if she didn't respond. She continued,

> The whole situation was incredible. Helene threatened to sue and expose me if I didn't turn over my own material to her. It was nuts. She had spent a few hours with me but had contributed nothing of value to my work. And, what made it even more painful, when she stayed with me, I had revealed some very personal information. My marriage was ending and I had just taken a lover. So I guess she thought she could both intimidate and blackmail me.

Lana turned the whole matter over to her attorney. She never did send Helene the notes and tapes; she gave them to her attorney with instructions to counter sue if necessary. At this point, it's unlikely the matter will go further.

The experience was costly for Lana—both in legal expenses and emotional pain. Though Helene could have done little with Lana's original material, most likely she felt rejected when Lana wrote to her saying they could not work together on the project. This example clearly shows how pain . . . turned to anger . . . can result in revenge that's destructive, unreasonable, and expensive.

You Wanted It, But You Didn't Get It

The following story offers two examples of revenge gone awry, and shows how revenge serves no constructive purpose. It can backfire and often does, hurting the perpetrators, and Danielle and Kimberly found out.

They both worked as secretaries in a large law firm in Denver, Colorado. Both had been with the firm for several years and decided there had to be more to life than being a secretary. An interoffice job-posting memo passed across their desks. The posting that caught their eyes was for an administrative assistant. What great news. An administrative assistant made more money than they did and got an added week of vacation. And prestige came with the new title.

With memo in hand, Danielle approached her boss and asked him to recommend her for the position. He said he could understand her desire to significantly increase her salary and get the extra vacation time, but he could not recommend her for the position because it required someone who was a self-starter and could work independently. He also said the job entailed a heavier workload. He then remarked that he was generally satisfied with her work, but he sometimes had to remind her to complete a job on time. He noted that she had gotten help from other secretaries in the office to meet her deadlines several times.

He then gave her some organizational tips to help prepare her to move up the career ladder. He also gave her some special projects that she could finish independently to get the feel of the extra work she could expect. After three months, he would gladly sit down and review her work. At that time, if appropriate, he would make the recommendation for her promotion, but not until she succeeded with the tasks he identified.

Kimberly's boss, on the other hand, enthusiastically supported her desire to move on and achieve more. On his recommendation, she got the position as administrative assistant. She was thrilled with the increased salary, added vacation time, and new title.

But Kimberly's triumph turned to discontent within a few months. Her old boss had neglected to equate her abilities to the responsibilities of the new job. She felt she was now too overworked and didn't have enough time to do anything. She grumbled about all the new projects coming her way.

Danielle let her discontent be known much sooner than Kimberly. She felt that her boss had unjustly criticized her work habits and products. She concluded the only reason he did not recommend her for the promotion was because he did not want to train a new secretary.

Both women showed their discontent by becoming roadblocks. Phone messages were lost; meetings for their bosses "accidentally" didn't get scheduled. They both took to bad mouthing their bosses to anyone within earshot.

Office morale got so low that the managing partner of the law firm stepped in and brought both situations to a head. In separate dealings with the women's bosses, he boldly told them to see to it their staff members either shaped up or shipped out. In the end, Danielle was terminated and Kimberly was demoted. Eventually she left the firm, too.

Both women displayed self-defeating behavior. Danielle was angry because she felt she had been passed over. Kimberly felt she was being put upon by doing more work than she thought she should be required to do. When they sought revenge against their respective bosses, they both suffered the consequences.

If you are stuck in a scenario that frustrates you and

causes anger to build, address the problem post haste rather than seek revenge. Certainly these examples show using revenge escalates the problem. Step back from the feelings and find time to strategize different ways to confront the issues. If you are able to identify what the problem is (and most definitely if you are *not* able to), enlist the input of a trusted friend, colleague, or relative. After all, your anger and frustration may prevent you from seeing the whole picture. You need feedback from someone who has no personal involvement. A cool head is the answer.

Hear No Evil, Speak No Evil

One of the most common forms of revenge is gossip. I guess that only a hermit is safe from gossip; it occurs in the workplace, in the neighborhood, even in the family. I've often said gossip can be likened to a pool . . . and not a sparkling emerald pool that you exercise in or cool off in to get refreshed during the scorching heat of summer. No, the gossip pool is like a cesspool filled with slime and sludge. And once you hop in, it is harder and harder to get the smell and the unpleasantness out of your life.

Now, gossip can be positive when it involves sharing anecdotes of another's admitted faux pas and foibles. In fact, many women use it as a way to connect or bond with other women. For some, gossip can even be a way to enhance self-esteem and confidence. However, when you publicize a confidential tidbit with the belief that, by sharing the information, your standing will be enhanced in another's eyes—be aware you will shine only temporarily. You've jumped into the cesspool. And, now that you are a known gossiper, you've become a prime target for more gossip.

What if you find yourself the target of someone's vengeful tongue? Rumors or innuendoes circulate among your friends, colleagues, co-workers, and family members. Now in harm's way, you must address and confront the gossip directly.

Take action by identifying the people who make the rounds of the gossip circles, then say something like: "Do you have any idea who could have started such an outrageous statement or rumor?" The tone should be one of incredulity—questioning, not accusatory.

When you find yourself the target of malicious gossip, make it clear you won't tolerate it. If you don't confront gossip, your silence acknowledges the truth of it. In Chapter 6, you read about the perils of being too nice and not wanting to confront. Do you see that both traits are self-sabotaging?

Of course, the reverse is true. If you listen to gossip without expressing your disgust about spreading unfounded rumors (or have become an Olympic medallist in the sport of gossip), you could be sabotaging yourself. How? When you spread gossip, whether true or untrue, you give off signals that you are not strong enough to take a stand against those who pass gossip to you. You are guilty by association when you condone it. It leads to others questioning your integrity.

When I was young we played a game called "Telephone." Some of my friends called it "Buzz." One player starts the game by whispering a story to the player on the right, and this story telling continues around the circle of players. When all players had heard the whispered message, the starter and the finisher recounted what had been said. Rarely did the message recounted by the finisher sound anything like the original version. We all thought it hilarious!

This happens in real life today. Each person's perception of what they hear is different and memory of what was said can be faulty. You could be credited with a real whopper!

Feathers in the Air

How damaging can gossip be? I love to use analogies to get my point across. Consider this one. You have a large goose down pillow on your bed. Your five-year-old's curiosity gets the best of her and she uses scissors to cut it open. When you arrive on the scene, feathers are everywhere.

Hoping to salvage your favorite pillow, you begin to gather them up in a vain effort to re-stuff the pillow, grumbling at your youngster all the while. It's an impossible task and even the vacuum chokes to death in its effort to help. Three months later, feathers are still surfacing.

Gossip is just like that. Once it's out in the open and starts to circulate, it's impossible to recall and erase everything that was said. The damage is done.

What, Who, How & When

When faced with tough situations, your brain can feel like a caged squirrel running around and around on its wheel. And you're getting nowhere fast. More thinking about the problem will give you a headache. So let's do some de-squirreling exercises. Start by writing it all down—*every* feeling, *every* incident, and *every* player. Your lists can be as long or short as you want.

What's going on in *(Your Name)* 's life today?
> What activities make me comfortable and uncomfortable in my life today? Rate each as a positive influence or negative, with plus or minus. Include all facets of your life.

Who are the people active in my life today?

> Who are the people that make me comfortable and uncomfortable in my life today? Rate each as a positive or negative influence with a plus or minus. Don't forget anyone.

How can I be more comfortable with the situations and people in my life?

> Separate each of the two lists above into two lists: pluses and minuses. Then rate each item on the new lists with a numerical rating.

When can I begin to make sense of the people and situations in my life?

Now that you've cleared every rotten piece of this mess out of your brain, take a break. Leave it alone for a day or two, then make any additions and corrections. At this time, follow these two important steps.

1. Identify the four top-rated plus activities and people in your life today. Commit to spending as much time as possible with them for at least 30 days.
2. Identify the four top-rated minus activities and people in your life today. Commit to spending as little time (or none) as possible with either of them for at least 30 days—*no* revenge for 30 days.

Don't misinterpret this. I'm not saying you should quit your job or volunteer work and play golf or tennis every day. I am saying if you concentrate on the positive elements in your life, you may find the negative ones aren't really the problems you thought they were. Plus, you've given yourself a time out from fretting and worrying. Hopefully, you can think more clearly.

When the month is over, look over the minus list carefully and make a plan to solve each problem that still exists. Give each a time line that requires some steady work from you. This will bring a resolution.

If you don't want to "go it alone" and believe someone else's opinion would help, get a trusted colleague or friend involved. Because your feedback partner knows you so well, some components of your lists are not new. Ask him or her to review your rated lists to see if you have included and rated everything and everyone correctly.

You want frankness and honesty from this partner. No holds barred. Your job is to listen to the feedback. Granted, you may discount some of it, but I recommend you pay attention and take meaningful notes. There's an old saying my grandmother often used, "If we but had the gift to see ourselves as others see us." Sometimes our perceptions are not fully accurate, thus feedback can be very valuable.

When you feel caught in a situation in which revenge becomes the guiding light, be sure to get a trusted opinion on the matter. The alternative—acting on revengeful feelings—sets you up for failure.

JB's Keeper #16
Revenge is sweet in the short term only.
Most likely, you end up the loser.

Chapter Fifteen

 Procrastination—
Abandon It!

You have, I have, everyone has indulged in the Scarlet O'Hara, "I'll think about it tomorrow" syndrome. Procrastination. It can sabotage relationships, careers, and even your time off. You have heard the excuses, and most likely used a few of them yourself:

> I'll do it later.
> I don't have the time.
> It can wait until _____ .
> Maybe. I'll think about it.

Procrastination is often veiled in plausible explanations (excuses), so it is comfortable to delay making a commitment or a decision. Many procrastinate because of fear . . . fear that they will fail or make a mistake. Some procrastinate because they are on a self-destruct course;

they actually *want* to fail. Others procrastinate because they do not want to be viewed negatively or criticized.

Procrastination can be an excuse *not* to do something. If you put off the action long enough, someone else may do the project for you. You rationalize that if someone else does it and it doesn't work out, you can say you're sure glad you didn't make such a bad mistake, or you knew it shouldn't have been done in the first place.

Anyone who procrastinates avoids action for a reason. Avoidance rationale includes phrases like: "This is not a priority, it is an unpleasant undertaking" or "I don't know how to do it and I am overwhelmed." And, believe it or not, some people procrastinate because they fear success. If they succeed, more may be expected of them.

Procrastination is the parent of internal conflict. You know you should probably do something about the situation, but the conflict within presents a phantom roadblock. The longer the problem is avoided, the greater you resist doing anything. When resistance matures and takes the place of procrastination, the problem or project gets permanently shelved. Your tap dance worked; postponement becomes your middle name.

The proficient procrastinator is headed directly for personal and career suicide, and death will be slow and painful. A procrastinator's speech is littered with phrases like: "If only . . ." or "I can't afford to" or "I'll get around to it one of these days" or "I don't have the time" etc. Bite your tongue the next time you are tempted to mouth anything similar. Dispose of all the "round-to-its" in your life. What is a round-to-it? All those things you've avoided doing that prickle your conscience because you didn't get around to it.

A classic example of procrastination tempts millions of

Americans every year. It's called April 15th—time to file your income tax return. Many routinely ask for extensions only because they put off sitting down to do it. Others perceive themselves to be so busy, they don't have time—tomorrow is another day. The only time this attitude really works is if you really *are* too busy; you know you will have to make time in one of your tomorrows. Yet how many ask for extensions when they are owed a refund?

Putting off making a decision today doesn't make it easier to do in one of your tomorrows. If applying for that job or joining that committee could enhance your present position—don't think about it tomorrow—go for it now.

Out of Balance

For Dan, an insurance agent, his life overwhelms him. He teeters on the edge of balance because of all the demands in his life: those at home, those of his aging parents and in-laws and those of his business. He works out of his home and rarely takes time to play. Dan puts off many things because he believes he doesn't have enough time in his day. Here's what he said,

> If I had more balance in my life, I would have more energy. I would have more time for my family, my wife, my parents and in-laws, and more time for my work. My office is in my home, and that's a problem. It's hard to keep away from my computer work when it's just a room away.
>
> If only I weren't so busy, I could enjoy where I live on five beautiful acres of land. I am surrounded by nature, and I like watching the birds. But I

rarely get to go out into the backyard. I know my physical well being isn't as good as it could be. I think about taking walks in the morning, but I just don't have time.

If only I weren't so busy, I could accept more opportunities to conduct seminars. Just the other day, I had to cancel a presentation because my parents needed me to take them for a doctor's appointment. They are important to me, so I deal with the added complexities.

Added complexities or no priorities? Dan has allowed himself to be stretched in too many directions. It's amazing if he knows whether it's morning or evening. No one can quarrel with his desire to help his aging parents. But he really should have taken the time to consider alternatives before he canceled the seminar that would help his business. By assisting his parents, he may have lost the confidence of some of his customers and may have lost out on some new contacts. A simple solution would have been to reschedule the appointment for his parents to accommodate his schedule.

Dan has a unique problem. It's one faced by most self-employed business people who work from their homes—people think they are always available because they don't have to ask the boss for time off. His family probably doesn't have a clue that he needs more time for himself and his business. Why has he procrastinated about having an organizational powwow with the family to discuss the needs of each member? And why, if he's concerned about his own health, does he refuse to allocate time to exercise or stretch?

In Dan's situation, he needs to do some prioritizing

and determine what is *really important* to him. He cannot continue the daily swings back and forth between family and business and keep his sanity, too. He has to commit. He has to give himself permission to get on with a life for himself.

If his business is important, he needs to concentrate on business development areas. He should also concentrate on ways to streamline his operation both to allow for growth and give his time to feed his psyche with free time and exercise. I suggested he drive out to the end of the acreage with his wife each morning when she leaves at seven o'clock for her job. Then he could walk back to the house, get his exercise and see birds along the way.

If he opts to be there for his aging parents and in-laws as a priority, he will have to decide that his business takes a back seat. Dan—and many others—habitually take a myopic approach, putting off decisions, then rationalizing and justifying why they can't do something. Dan should call a halt to everything for a few days to prioritize and make a plan that will stick.

Procrastinators Are Not Alone

If you are a procrastinator, you are not alone. Every March, the Procrastinators' Club of America holds its annual meeting in celebration of National Procrastination Week! Procrastinating is not new. Famous procrastinators include Greek philosopher Hippocrates who said, "To do nothing is also a good remedy." Author James Thurber had a different twist, saying, "It is better to have loafed and lost than never to have loafed at all."

There are times that each of us drags our feet. Some do it more than others. Below are several styles of procrastinating. Where do you fit in?

6 Styles of Procrastination

Type	Character	Thinking	Speaking	Acting	Need
Perfectionist	Critical	All-or-Nothing	I should/ I have to	Impeccable	Control
Dreamer	Flighty	Vague	I wish/ Someday	Passive	Being Distinctive
Worrier	Security	Fearful Fretful	Vacillating	What if?	Careful
Rebellious	Resistant Pig-headed	Contrasting	Pissy	Defiant	Different
Crises	Moody	Frantic	Absolutes	Dramatic or Withdraw	Attention
Overachiever	Hectic	Duty-bound	Can't say no	Can do Anything	Confident

Steps to Overcoming Procrastination

The previous chart can direct you to insights about your own procrastination style. Whatever that style is, these steps will help you overcome your excuses and get on with it!

1. *Ask yourself what the problem is.*

   First, be aware you are procrastinating and be willing to define what the problem is.

2. *Prioritize, prioritize, prioritize.*

   Determine what activities are most important to you and do them first. You make prioritizing decisions all the time; become more conscious and deliberate with them.

3. *Start with a small chunk.*

   When you come across a project that seems overwhelming, instead of the standard, "I'll do this tomorrow," start doing it in chunks.

4. *Check your attitude and change your words.*

   Your attitude is a strong factor. To change your attitude and behavior, practice rephrasing your thoughts and responses. When you think "wish," substitute the word "will." "Try to" (instead of "like to" and "want to") is preferred over "have to."

5. *Get rid of the "round-to-its" in your life.*

   Remember that a "round-to-it" represents all those things you've avoided doing that prickle your conscience because you didn't get around to it. You don't need them.

6. *Reward yourself.*

Trainers of both human and animal behavior quickly learn that when the subjects "perform" as directed, they receive a reward. When you overcome areas in which you procrastinate, it is time for a "bravo." Give yourself a reasonable time limit to accomplish your task and, when successful, break out the reward. You get to choose what it is!

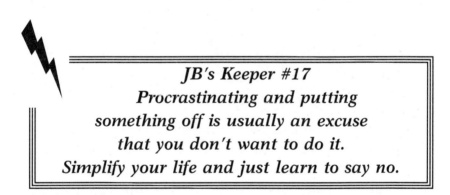

JB's Keeper #17
Procrastinating and putting
something off is usually an excuse
that you don't want to do it.
Simplify your life and just learn to say no.

Chapter Sixteen

 You Can't Do It All—
Superwoman and
Superman Are Myths

Are you worn out? If you are like most, your day runs out before you get everything done that you want or need to. Today, everyone is simply overloaded. You have extra pressures from balancing family and workplace or community responsibilities as well as your own personal life. Does that sound like you?

Because you are overloaded, you experience stress, anger, resentment, worry, illness, frustration, and, most of all, exhaustion. Sometimes separately; sometimes in combinations; even, sometimes, all of the above.

Working the Second Shift

In the nineties, Patricia Ulbrich, University of Akron (Ohio), analyzed data from a national study she conducted of 1246 couples. Household chores were a key concern. Her study revealed that women differed widely on how much time they spent doing chores. Some append a few hours a week; others turned household chores into another full-time job. Ulbrich found that:

✓ Women who work outside their home for 35 or more hours a week spend an average of 26 hours a week on housework.
✓ Women who are employed outside the home for fewer than 35 hours a week spend 33.8 hours a week on housework.
✓ Women who identified themselves primarily as home-makers spend an average of 38.5 hours a week on housework.

In other words, it doesn't matter if you work inside or outside the home, the time dedicated to keeping the house up is about the same— *the average woman does 32.3 house of housework a week*. And that doesn't include childcare. The woman who identifies herself as a homemaker usu-ally dedicates a considerable amount of time toward com-munity, school, and charitable projects. It's no wonder a woman's work is never done.

So what is the man's contribution around the house? Men devote an average of 8.7 hours a week for household chores. In some cases, men do nothing, and in others, they contribute greatly to running the household.

Other studies have shown that when a woman comes home from a "pay" job, she starts another shift. When she is married or living with a partner, the partner-spouse enjoys R&R status, for the most part. Meanwhile, women proceed with their domestic shift: kids, cooking, cleaning, and errands.

Women tend to experience the pressure of maintaining a social and home life. When men begin their career advancement, they commonly find support from their wives or girlfriends. Another study at the same time revealed that married men make more money when their wives don't work for pay. Domestic chores are taken care of, and wives are more willing to be patient when their husbands travel on business or put in extra hours at the office.

The working woman who is married—whether at a managerial, executive, or non-management level—rarely has that luxury or support. Most of the time, she also does most of the domestic work. If single, a woman usually discovers that potential mates resent her time commitments. She may have trouble establishing a relationship, or she may even decide not to enter into one because she doesn't have time to develop it. Relationships take work.

Superwoman Is Pooped

So, what is a woman to do? Can she have it all? Most women who have some maturity—usually women over 45—will tell you it is possible to have it all. It is, though, impossible to have it all at once. Most women tried to be every thing to every body and many suffered the consequences. Now, we realize it's not healthy, it's not fair, and it's not realistic. But many still continue to do "it."

Doing "it" literally means you do too much. One of my button pushers was an ad for Enjoli perfume, the one that gloated, "I can bring home the bacon, fry it up in the pan, and never, ever, let you forget I'm a woman." How many women do you know come through the door, grab a frying pan that sparkles, whip up dinner for the kids, change their clothes, look like they stepped off the cover of *Glamour* magazine with perfect make-up and hair, then trot out for a romantic evening of dinner and dancing with their man?

Madison Avenue and the media must get real. Most

women would probably prefer to soak in a tub when they get home. Frying bacon and bogeying into the night is most likely very low on the "to do" list. If a woman averages 32.3 hours of housework a week, she needs to hit the floor running when she walks through that door (or gets out of bed).

The "Doing It All" Myth

Years ago, I was interviewed by a national women's magazine. Somewhere the editors learned that I worked more than 40 hours a week, had three children, was married, got involved in the community, and sat on several boards. In other words, they wanted to know how I did it all. When they called for the interview, I told them what allowed me to do as much as I did do was getting help. I paid for it.

That was the wrong answer; it was not what they wanted to hear. In fact, it's the first interview I felt I really "flunked." As we pursued the conversation further, I learned what the interviewer wanted me to say—that I cooked and baked on weekends, late in the evening when I got home and/or when I got up early in the morning. The fruits of my late-night endeavors would be frozen so my family would have casseroles, goodies, and snacks when the need arose. I remember telling her I loved to cook and bake, but doing so for the mere sake of stocking up the freezer wasn't the objective, ever.

When she described the demographics for the magazine, my response was, "It sounds like the average woman. Why don't you do this average woman a favor and map out a strategy and plan? Show her how and why she should get some help if she is putting in the 40-hour week working outside the home." Her response was, "No!

The magazine couldn't do that. " She really wanted to write about Superwoman.

Well, women can't do it all at the same time, or have it all at once. Women can do it all over a period of time, in bits and pieces. Magazines and TV shows do such an incredible disservice to their readers, viewers, and listeners with such poppycock. Women do not need more responsibilities and obligations piled on them. They need help prioritizing so that there can be some balance in the day, including time for them. And women need to say "No" more often.

According to the Bureau of Labor Statistics and the National Commission of Children, more than 60 percent of married mothers work outside the home and have children under the age of six. More than six million single mothers are in the workplace. For most women today, homemaking and working are not either/or life-styles. Women's lives are more highly individualized, with roles changing from week to week and month to month.

It is meaningless to label some women as homemakers and others as workers. Every woman works! It's also important to delete outdated and unrealistic terms that throw us back into the "nostalgic" times of *Ozzie and Harriet, Donna Reed,* and *Leave It To Beaver.* I would even include the latest most perfect family in which both parents worked outside the home, the Huxtables, in *The Cosby Show.* Few women really want to live these stereotypes.

Sure, life in the '50s, for families at least, had a slower pace. There was a greater sense of community and many enjoyed a middle class lifestyle with a single income to support the family. But there was a cost: men and women had to follow the rules. Women stayed home, men went to work, women cared for the men and the family, and men financially supported the family's lifestyle. That was it— no variables.

Instead of bemoaning how things used to be, it's far more logical to look at how things are today . . . and how we want to shape them as we go forward into the future.

Two Common Factors

Some advertisements are beginning to reflect that we are not in the *Ozzie and Harriet* and *Leave It To Beaver* era. That's good news. If you viewed those two TV series—as I did growing up plus watching syndicated re-runs—you would probably be surprised by your attitude change. When I saw a few episodes recently, I was amused at how incredibly boring those households could be at times.

AT&T aired an ad campaign that showed a professional woman chatting on a cellular phone. The ad's unexpected setting was the bleacher seats at her child's sporting event. McDonald's also came up with an ad campaign in the mid-'90s showing a single mom arriving home exhausted on a rainy night. When she gets there, her daughter reminds her of a promised meal at McDonald's. Giving in, as lots of moms do, they set out. On the way, mom tells her daughter about her day at the office.

Some advertisers try to find a commonality or bond between the homemaker and the woman who works outside the home. Two common factors, I believe, are obvious: women are under stress, and most women need help. Ask any mother who is trying to juggle her time each day around kids who are under the age of five and underfoot. Ask a woman who is dropping off and picking up kids at day care, and also has to manage meetings and appointments. Or ask a woman who doesn't have children and/or is single about others' expectations and perceptions that infer she has the freedom to be available for extra work.

Today's woman is far busier than her counterpart of any of the previous decades. She has so many more roles to play in her family life, her social life, and—if she works outside the home—her work life. Granted, the woman who lived in the Wild West in the 1800s and 1900s spent a long and grueling day making soap and candles, churning butter, plowing, canning—just surviving. She wasn't, though, interrupted with the demands of phones, carpooling, crime, drugs, neighbors, keeping-up-with-the-Jones pressure that a lot of women experience today. Well, you might have seen her pile the kids into the wagon and pool to the schoolhouse. But the rest of the problems didn't exist. Let's just say that having a "traditional wife" would do wonders for most women (and men).

Everyone Could Use a Wife

Unfortunately, most women don't have them; even some men question whether they really have wives, at least in the traditional *Ozzie and Harriet* style. Research from the early '90s has shown that men would actually work fewer hours if they had their "druthers." They don't mind the 40-hour-a-week job; it's the 50 and 60-hour-plus weeks demanded of them. Their employers require it, and it's still one of the standard unwritten rules.

As enlightened as many people feel they are, most jobs are still designed for men as the primary breadwinner and for women as the primary domestic laborer in the home (which they are). Many believe if there were adequate child care facilities, problems for woman at work would be minimal. Maybe. But, it's not that simple and it's not the final solution to the problem that women face—being overloaded, overworked, and, at times over-stressed.

It is important to acknowledge that many husbands help their wives with domestic obligations. But few do it on a 50/50 basis. Sometimes, women's ideas of a domestic collaboration don't pan out. When husbands don't participate to the degree their wives feel they should, women commonly protect themselves from their disappointment and frustration by covering up for them.

What happens? Many wives actually give their husbands more credit for what they contribute to household work and childcare tasks than they actually do. Some women won't let go of domestic chores when a partner wants to help—territories surface. In some cases, women become enablers and co-dependents—supporting their spouses' domestic laziness and/or shortcomings. Internal reactions—or sometimes reactions shared with those outside the family—spill over into anger.

Standing Up For Your Needs

I "flunked" the interview with the national magazine—the one that wanted me to say that I worked extra hours baking, cooking, and freezing. They refused to hear that I got help. When I told them one of the best things they could advise was to get/buy help, they rejected me. It didn't fit the belief systems of their readers. Chances are, most do tasks that are unnecessary or could be deferred to a later time. Better yet, could be completed by hiring someone to help—if they would only give themselves permission.

From the years of 1972 through 1986, I did financial consulting. Routinely, my clients would tell me their money ran out before the end of the month. When we opened the checkbooks and added their ATM withdrawals, we determined the total they spent. Usually, we found monies I identified as "kiss-off" funds. I suspect you have some, too.

I suggest you re-route your "kiss-off" dollars. The first

step is to identify your priorities. Then use these dollars to take more time for yourself and those you care about. Here are some ideas for having fun at a low cost: movies (go out and rent one to view with a friend), books (pick up a good one at your library where books, even the latest best-sellers, are free), shoes and clothing (shop at discount or near-new stores to get more for your money). Or with your "kiss-off" funds, you could buy some help, and plan some "kiss-off" time and money. Ten minutes and $10 here and there add up.

When women find themselves in the workplace, their lives at home don't change much. Housework and child-raising responsibilities remain theirs. Why is this? Do men conspire to keep them barefoot and pregnant, or do women secretly yearn to be taken care of by men? I don't think so.

The disparity is really rooted in the conflicts of work and family life. Women attempt too much because they think many domestic chores are "women's work" . . . and because women don't have "wives" to do all the things that "need" to be done. I believe it's time that women step up and ask for what they need.

If you have kids and work outside your home, you may find that your workplace is not set up to meet the demands of a working mother. If a new baby arrives and you elect to take time off, you may encounter some form of economic shortfall or even banishment to the so called Mommy Track. And, if a woman does not take time off, guaranteed she is going to be exhausted. Any guilt from not being with the family's latest addition only adds icing to an already toxic cake.

Sharing "Mom" Stuff

More women are starting small businesses from their homes. Loretta has been self-employed for many years.

Many, including her children and her husband, assumed that she could take time off at a moment's notice because she didn't punch a time clock or report to a boss.

She didn't realize how much of her work day was spent doing non-work related items—running errands and picking up kids—until her husband took early retirement. He now had the time to work with her in her business. She shares that this past year has been her business' best ever. When I spoke to her, her husband was doing "Mom" stuff. He had left the office that afternoon, for example, to take their daughter to get her driver's license. Loretta explained,

> It's been real interesting. I didn't realize how much that type of thing—taking the kids to get driver's licenses, going for dentist appointments, etc.— dragged me down. Any type of outside commitment takes time, but I didn't realize how much time until he started doing it.
>
> We are still working on sharing chores and activities when I'm home. We both come home from work, presumably together, or at least follow each other in our cars. But he'll come in and sit down, and I'll be expected to get dinner ready. At one point I said, "How come I'm the only one in the kitchen, standing up, preparing food, and everyone else is sitting around doing nothing?"

No one has it all; there are going to be "give-ups" for both men and women. The having-it-all, doing-it-all, being-it-all mentality propels too many of us into a frenetic—almost insatiable—quest for even more. For many, it becomes impossible to celebrate the victories along the way. Many men will admit today that they don't have it all. They just don't talk about it as openly as women do.

Balancing Your Life

When I talk about the need to prioritize and get balanced in my workshops, I have my audience do a simple exercise. It involves taking a piece of paper and tearing it into four parts. On each part, participants write a word or phrase that identifies one of the top four issues that are currently important to them. It could be going back to school, changing jobs, getting married, getting unmarried, starting an exercise program, spending an extra hour each day with children, and so on. You name it, we all have lists of wishes we'd like to do.

What are your top four? Take a few minutes and write them down. After you have identified the four most important items in your life, look them over. Remove the least important of the four. Again, scan the remaining three. Remove the next one that is least important. Of the two remaining, put aside the one that is less important. You have one left. The question becomes: do you spend time each day, focusing, concentrating, supporting, encouraging, what is written on your single piece of paper?

Now, a small percentage in my audiences nod their heads saying that, yes, indeed they do. But most don't. If you don't nod your head yes, maybe you're not sure. Or perhaps you tell yourself you would like to spend more time on that item. Then it's time for "time out." If you try to be all things to all people, you can be described in one word: exhausted. And, not so smart.

If you work full-time and do your average of 32-plus hours of housework a week, when will you find the time to dedicate to the top four items that are important to you?

If you are not dedicating some time each day so you can knock off the number one priority on your list and go on to number two, etc., then you need to become myopic and say No to as many things as is humanly possible. Yes, you're going to disappoint some people—too bad. You will have the time for your priorities and possibly more energy to meet the demands you turned down for a while. The key is to be selective.

Turning "No" into Your Partner

Several factors will assist you in bringing balance into your life; the first is to say No. Everyone has taken on commitments and projects they wished they had never heard of. In fact, sometimes we agree to do something just because we've been worn down by the proponent. Then we swear that will be the last committee we will work on—until the next one comes along. Say no.

Saying no to unfair practices in your workplace counts, too. If you haven't already, begin now to educate—bring pressure on—decision-makers in your workplace. Demand more flexibility. Encourage your employer to give credit for part-time work and shared work. Definitely pool sick days, vacation days, and personal days off and put them all into a bank-type of account. You can add days (deposit) or use days (withdraw) to meet your goals.

Get help. If you have to buy it, trade it, or enlist your kids and/or spouse, do it now. Don't make excuses or rationalize when other members in the household don't help. When you do, you will be less overwhelmed, more responsive, happier, and healthier. Call it balanced.

JB's Keeper #18
If you don't say NO, your Yeses
become worthless.

Chapter Seventeen

Perfection—Take the Pressure off Yourself

"If you can't do the job right, don't do it at all." Is this motto one that characterizes you or anyone in your life? Take comfort in knowing you are not alone; millions deal with this phenomenon daily. I am talking about perfection.

Perfection is, to some, a virtue. For others, it's a nemesis. To achieve real perfection, you need to be incredibly focused and let nothing or no one get in the way of achieving your current goal. A person thus dedicated is driven, almost haunted, by an inability to stop working until a job is completed. This can be hard on the perfectionist and everyone around her.

The possibility of finding errors or omissions drives perfectionists to bury themselves in their task—permission to make a mistake is never granted. They are proud of their virtuous hard work and attention to every detail. More often than not, they give far more than was ever asked or expected of them. Some call them "control freaks."

The Dark Side of Perfection

When anything—in this case, the need to be perfect—becomes an obsession, it also flirts with addiction. Perfectionists become addicted to details—no detail goes unnoticed, no matter how infinitesimal it is. Minor details take on unjustifiable importance, then grow out of proportion to the big picture. And, because perfectionists fail to see the big picture, they're stunned to find they may have been excluded from it.

Why? Because of their myopic approach. Perfectionists spend so much time getting things right, they lose sight of their overall efficiency. Sure, they may be getting the job done because most perfectionists work long hours. But as a result, they are exhausted and don't have a life outside the work they are attempting to perfect. Most perfectionists play catch-up. They are always one step behind and out of sync with the areas of their lives they don't have time for; they live in the myopic mode.

Flexibility is not in the lexicon of the perfectionist. Those in the throes of perfectionism have ruled out the possibility of choice—there is but one focus. They are so busy doing "it" right that much in life passes them by. New challenges and opportunities can be missed because the perfectionist doesn't have time to incorporate them. Instead, others with fewer skills and a lesser need for perfection can jump, unchallenged, at new opportunities.

In these situations, the perfectionist is left eating the dust of those who are not so picky. How do the less-than-perfect ones do? They may make mistakes, but they have impressed others that they are flexible risk takers and team players. They have demonstrated their willingness to learn new things, though they don't have the proven skills. And they learn that, as time progresses, a mistake will not devastate them.

Let's pause here to review some characteristics—both positive and negative—of the perfectionist. Striving for a little more perfection may have some value for you.

Single Mindedness—Focus

Negative: Perfectionists will not permit outside influences, including other people, to interfere with their concept (focus) of how something is to be done and when. They are inflexible about the methods used to accomplish the goal or task at hand. No one can do anything right except them, so delegation is maddeningly difficult. A perfectionist must always be in control.

Positive: Focus is the key element in getting something done correctly, be it big or small. Flexibility—a challenge for a perfectionist—is the necessary buffering agent to focus. The input and help of others can usually enhance a job well done. Then it becomes a win-win: you're right and they are, too.

Hard Working—Intense

Negative: Perfectionists are hard workers; they almost invariably produce quality work when they finally deliver it. They get to the top of the heap quicker than most because they work longer hours than others can or will. They see little virtue in recreation activities but, when they do play, they must win. They are rarely characterized as "co-operative" or "team players"—they are intense.

Positive: Productivity at work, at home, and at play is a major concern. Deep down, they want to be good (close to perfect) in all areas. It's helpful for perfectionists to be willing to put in some extra hours in the weaker areas to balance their overall position.

The successful person who is also happy and balanced takes time to evaluate the day which has passed, and plan for the one to come. Yes, they work hard but they use their time wisely. They intensely get the most out of life.

Never Satisfied—Never Finished

Negative: Perfectionists are slaves to detail. This slavery is often the result of a fear of failure. Many perfectionists fear failure and the possibility of criticism so much, they have a hard time saying "it's finished." They can maintain their power only if a project is never completed. Or, if completion is a must, the perfectionist positions someone else as the scapegoat for any errors or omissions, then says, "I really wasn't satisfied."

Positive: Planning and attention to detail in all areas of life will serve perfectionists well. Fear of failure is natural but shouldn't immobilize. Though perfectionists may not be able to satisfy everyone including themselves, getting the "dratted" job done is an achievement in itself. It is most important to learn from previous errors.

Critical

Negative: Perfectionists find things to criticize that few people ever give credence to. Always right, they will argue a point to the death—often using fuzzy logic that is confusing and confounding. If they didn't do it, it wasn't done right. And, if you hear a rare word of praise from them, it's usually couched with their observation of something that could have done better. They—and they alone—wear the crown of perfection.

Positive: Everyone likes to hear a well-deserved word of praise. Perfectionists should strive to be good receivers and givers of praise . . . and not lose sight of making improvements to become the best possible along the way.

Balance is Possible

The desire for perfection can be healthy; it's the key to balance. The perfectionist has to step away from the attitude of "all or nothing"—the self-sabotage feeling that if the entire project can't be completed and completed correctly, it's not worthwhile.

When I was working on my doctorate, one of the professors asked us to correlate the quality of completed assignments with how much time was spent on them. An important concept was explored that day. The quality of one's work product is not always the result of the time spent. I reported that the quality of what I did (that is, my grade) was high. But because of my other obligations and responsibilities, I could not dedicate a great portion of my day to class work. When I said this to my professor, he glared at me. "Ms. Briles," he said, "you could be a star. Given the quality of work you produce, if you would just commit a little more time, you would be at the top." I suspect that he was right, but I didn't have the time to find out. I was already stretched to the breaking point; I had to set limits.

I learned to set limits, thanks to another professor I had. He taught a course in strategic planning. "In business," he said, "there are some times when you are going to have to take some short cuts. You will have to make the decision of when something is good enough. Not perfect— but good enough."

Was it critical for me to have a 4.0 grade point average throughout my years of doctorate class work? No, not at all; 3.6 was good enough. I had many responsibilities besides my Ph.D. studies. I worked and I had a family. We were in the middle of a financial crisis. I couldn't and didn't attempt to do it all, much less do it perfectly. I refused to hang myself with the noose of perfection . . . which is sometimes easier said than done.

Letting Go Is Hard To Do

Sarah spent many years getting her education to become an engineer. When she joined a firm in 1977, women engineers were just starting to be hired. She is now married with two children. Her present company where she works part-time offers limited family benefits because most of the male decision-makers—both old-timers and newly hired— have stay-at-home wives.

Like most engineers, she wants to have a place for everything, and everything in its place. She carried into her work the perfectionist molding from her mom and that, in turn, overflowed into her home life. When kids came along, Sarah found chaos the norm in a very short period of time. Her challenge was twofold: having to be both perfect and in balance. Perfectionism had to be everywhere, yet it threw her out of balance. Here is what Sarah experienced,

I worked for the engineering firm for ten years before I had my first baby. I went right back to work and, two-and-a-half years later, my second son was born. After 15 years, I finally took a leave of absence from full-time work. I am now on my second year of leave. Before, I worked 40 to 50 hours a week at my profession; now, I work 10 to 15 hours a week and I'm a lot happier.

At the beginning of the new arrangement, I still went into work as if it was a regular day. It took me eight months to accept that I wasn't at work full-time. It was hard for me to let go. I'm a very private person; I want to have my house immaculate and everything in order. But I was exhausted going to work full-time, cleaning, organizing, being a mom, being a wife. Still, I didn't want anyone else to come in and do the cleaning for me.

I had requested this leave of absence because I found staying at work was more difficult with all these other outside factors demanding my attention. The leave made my life far simpler.

Advancing higher in the company was never an objective. I'm an extremely competent engineer. But that's not the primary factor if someone wants to move up. Values are placed on those who have skills I really don't possess . . . skills like speaking in front of large groups, being able to finesse difficult situations, and the like. I'm not really interested in acquiring them. So, my part-time arrangement works fine. I keep my foot in the door as a technical engineer, I'm stimulated when I work with peers, and I have my family. The balance has worked.

Sarah speaks to her perfectionist needs. She stated that her husband really didn't care what the house looked like. It could be disorganized and dirty; it didn't really matter to him. His attitude was, "If you want it nice, go ahead and do it; but if you don't, that's OK too." It was not a problem with him if she hired outside help. But, being the private perfectionist person she is, no one would really satisfy her. And that is an issue that perfectionists have to deal with.

The Perfectionist's Medal

Perfectionists are masters at micro-management. Simply put, this means control. Perfectionists want to control the process no matter what it is. At home, it is controlling everything—how the clothes are folded, how the dishes are put in the dishwasher, etc. In the work place, perfectionists are far more interested in how a co-worker or employee does the work instead of what the outcome is. They often wonder why no one really appreciates them enough to pin a medal on them.

The perfectionist is usually quite immune to words of praise. They can neither acknowledge praise for themselves, nor can they praise others. They always seem to find something wrong; they nit pick or minimize the efforts of others. Yet any psychologist or behaviorist would highly recommend using praise. It's not that a perfectionist doesn't believe in praise; they just believe it should be dispensed only when a job is done perfectly. And, since very few people are perfect except themselves, words of praise don't easily flow from their mouths.

Eliminating Perfectionism from Your Plate

When you are able to lessen your perfectionism style, you will lessen your fear and anxiety of "what if..." But be aware that when you first decide to back away from your position of being impeccable in every way, expect to experience an actual increase in your anxiety levels. This is a short-term reaction. Listen to soothing music or relaxation tapes, take an exercise or yoga class. Meditation and prayer can also provide great support.

Below are some steps you can incorporate into your "rejecting perfectionism" philosophy.

✓ *When you take a task on, set a definite time limit.*
    In most cases, when time is up, stop your project and take a breather. Come back to it in an hour; do a quick overview and determine if it is "good enough" to turn in or just needs minor tweaking. Don't keep doing it over and over.

✓ *Accept difficult projects.*
    A great deal of satisfaction is derived from the "process" of doing something. A more intricate task than you have done in the past may forge you into different venues of learning. Avoid your perfectionist mode and jump in.

✓ *Set goals.*
    With goals—no matter how big or small—it takes a series of steps. With each step, you have completed a component of the big picture—something a perfectionist has enormous difficulty in seeing. Your goal leads to the big picture.

✓ *Learn new things.*
    My fourth step to building confidence is to learn new things. It keeps your brain in gear and revitalizes your spirit. It may be trivial or quite intricate. Learning new tasks allows you to stumble a bit. After all, some of the greatest advancements have been made from a sea of mistakes. Start swimming.

✓ *Measure worry.*
    When approaching new tasks and skills, ask yourself, "On a scale of 1 to 10—with 10 being "absolute-

ly" and 1 being "no way"—will failing to be perfect on this cripple your career, destroy your relationships, or destroy you? If you score over 9, take a pass. Otherwise, roll up your sleeves and take a deep breath.

✓ **Overlook mistakes—yours and others.**

Reward yourself—and those you work and play with—even on minor issues. You no longer have to carry a critical tongue—one that rarely praises or rewards anyone, including yourself.

✓ **Develop a buddy system.**

We all need feedback. Identify someone you trust, and contact that person often. Between the two of you, work out a few signals that say, "Time out, the perfectionist is not in."

In 1971, my infant son died very suddenly. Because of that, I was shocked into learning something very important. I learned that the dust will be on the furniture tomorrow, the next day, next week, next month, next year . . . it never goes away. Just like Sarah, I used to want to have my house perfect . . . even though I had to take care of four kids under the age of eight. Can you imagine what huge amount of pressure I put on myself to act on my perfectionist tendencies while I was grieving and caring for small children? The person I am today wouldn't tolerate that kind of pressure. I suggest it would be senseless for you to attempt that, too.

Everyone needs to learn to delegate, to ask for help, and get it. If something has a few wrinkles, bumps, a typo or smudge, ask yourself these questions before you don your perfectionist apron. If this isn't perfect:

Will I lose my job or my position?
Will my marriage or relationship fall apart?
Will my friends and family desert me?
Will my health deteriorate?
Will I lose all my money?
Will my world fall apart?

I suspect your answer was No to each of the above. Does that mean you are uncomfortable not doing that task "just so?" Most likely you answered Yes. But you are learning new behaviors, new habits. Unless you have what I call a "cosmic goose"—an event that instantly changes your life as the death of my son did—it will take some time to evolve out of your perfectionist mode. Pat yourself on the back with each step you take.

JB's Keeper #19
Perfectionism is a form of procrastination.
If something is not right,
it has to be done over, and over—
delaying other tasks.

Chapter Eighteen

 Failure—The Key Is
to Learn from It

Years ago, I hosted a dinner party for the "girls"—long time friends who got together every few months just to catch up. The fall evening was beautiful, the food delicious and, as always, we had an animated reunion of friends.

Who were we? Four women who wore various professional hats: one headed up an advertising firm; another was quite high in state politics; one was in senior management with a prestigious Silicon Valley company; the fourth (me) owned a highly visible financial planning firm.

Each of us had succeeded in breaking through barriers before we had ever heard of the phrase "glass ceiling." Our conversation turned toward the many successes each of us had accomplished. For two of our group, success had come from creating and completing projects and products that had impacted a company's bottom line. One had received several offers to be CEO for other companies and the other had started her own company. Our politically savvy strategist had successfully backed several high profiled legislative bills and now was mayor of a large city. I had taken great pleasure in the resurrection of many old buildings that had been renovated to a new life.

As we talked, the subject of failure popped up. Did we have failures? You bet. We all felt we had more than our fair share. Let me introduce you to my friends, Charlene, Liz, and Lucy as I share their stories.

The CEO Gets Duped

Charlene was a dazzling financial strategist. She coordinated, developed and presented a major financing strategy which became a key factor in her company's positioning as a select member of the Fortune 100. Her skill and savvy attracted the attention of other companies. It wasn't long before she had job offers all across the country. Eventually, she accepted the position of CEO at a new start-up company in Northern California.

She said one of her most dismal personal failures centered on money—her own. She was duped by another woman who verbally, publicly, and visibly purported to support other women and their causes. Charlene headed a long list of victims. The magnitude of the problem surfaced when one of her colleagues began to recheck references. It became evident the woman had used multiple references—many of whom were among Charlene's circle of friends.

By the time Charlene realized that she was dealing with a con-artist that purported to be an avid supporter of women's events, the woman had bilked her out of more than $15,000. Charlene was horrified that she had been made to look stupid. She felt everyone knew of the duplicity—and her failure to thoroughly check out the woman's credentials.

Out On the Limb

Liz is a successful entrepreneur, heads up her own advertising agency. She took great pride in her ability to look out for the little guy, not letting the bullies of the workplace stomp on others. Before starting her own company, she was at the forefront of consciousness-raising within the corporation where she worked. She aided women who had been sexually harassed or targeted for discrimination in securing job promotions.

Commonly, other women would routinely seek her out for her no-nonsense, to-the-point advice on their problems. Over a period of time, their complaints became so overwhelming; she felt some action had to be taken.

Meeting with them, she identified their various complaints, and put them into categories. Approximately 25 women vowed to unite against the injustices inflicted upon them. Energy levels were high—Liz's co-workers asked her to act as their spokesperson. She agreed, feeling they were united in their purpose. Surprise, surprise. When she went forward, they went back. She was out on the limb, all alone.

For a variety of reasons, they all dropped out. Worrying about jobs, rocking the boat, just being busy were common excuses. Because Liz had been so vocal about the wrongful practices of the company, she found herself locked out. She got fired.

Ten years have passed since that incident, but Liz still feels the sting—and a sense of failure. She felt she should have anticipated the outcome before jumping into the frying pan. Then she could have avoided the heat she took.

Liz was angry with herself for misjudging the others' commitment to their cause.

One Vote Too Many

Lucy experienced one of the most public scandals. It was seeded shortly after she was elected mayor of a distinguished city. She was well liked, publicly acknowledged, and received respect nationally as well as within her own community. She and her husband had been long time residents and had built a successful business.

Shortly after her election, she was contacted by a woman who had been a very vocal political supporter of hers. But when Lucy refused to support several causes the woman tried to force on her, war was declared. Her old "supporter" became her enemy. Rumors, innuendoes, accusations, and downright lies about Lucy and her husband were circulated among local and state authorities.

It wasn't long before charges for "conduct unbecoming an elected official" were filed. Accusations of bribery and vote manipulation led the list. Lucy spent the next few years drowning in the justice system. Her name was smeared on the front pages of the newspaper, on TV, and radio.

In the third month of the trial, sanity returned to the scene. The state's attorneys basically said, "Your Honor, we have made a mistake. It appears that our chief witness has committed perjury at least 41 times! We would like to withdraw our charges."

Whoa—can you imagine being in Lucy's seat? Of course, she and her husband felt enormous relief. Their family and friends cheered. They had been vindicated— the state acknowledged they had made a mistake.

But—it was and still is a big "but"—what about Lucy and her family? She was forced out of and intimidated by prominent community boards; she was arrested and paraded in prison garb in front of TV cameras; her reputation in the community was trashed; her health took a nosedive; their house was sold to pay legal bills—a tidy sum of $350,000 plus.

A "We are sorry, your Honor, we have made a mistake" just doesn't seem to do it. Lucy and her family lost big time; the state, meaning the taxpayers, lost by spending money on a senseless and unfounded accusation; the community lost big because a strong and committed family pulled up roots and moved themselves and their business to another state. The losses Lucy and her family incurred are incalculable.

When failure faces you—especially a public one—it's hard to sort it out. Why did this happen? Did Lucy fail by not recognizing early on she had a potential enemy in the camp? Did she fail because of naiveté—this just couldn't be happening? Did she fail because she didn't take into consideration that anyone in politics is prone to attack? Did she fail because of the wild card of plain bad luck—being in the wrong place at the wrong time? Did she fail because she was just too trusting? Maybe all of the above and then some.

The Wrong Partner

All of us at our reunion had experienced professional and personal trauma; I was no exception. It extended to my family, my health, my friends, and my business. Failure turned my life upside down for more than 10 years. I first shared my story (as well as Lucy's) in my book *Woman to Woman*. It involved trust—the violation of it; money—the misuse of it; friendships—their termination; and talk—the spreading of rumors, mixed with malicious and devastating gossip.

In the '80s, I was in partnership with another woman. Our business was to rehab old buildings and convert them into bed-and-breakfast-type hotels. My partner was the contractor and developer for each project; I raised the money to fund them. Because of our track record, we easily borrowed construction loans from the bank to complete our projects.

One afternoon, I received a call from the banker. He requested my presence in his office promptly the next morning. I was told to bring an updated personal financial statement. During that meeting, I wanted to throw up. I learned that my partner and friend of several years misappropriated several hundred thousand dollars from the construction funds. My name was on the primary construction loan and I had personally guaranteed it. The bank wanted to know how I intended to pay it off and when.

After an extensive accounting probe, I knew everything was in jeopardy—the project, my business, and my hard-earned reputation. Like Lucy, I found myself being attacked by clients, friends, the media, even the regulatory agencies that monitor the securities industry. Almost $450,000 had vanished. One of my "favorite" bills was for landscaping—none had been done. Well, maybe a few flowerpots, but not $18,000 worth!

My partner was forced out. I now found myself running a small hotel—a situation I'm sure God never intended me to be in. Initially, I hired a general manager. We warded off the creditors for awhile. Before long, the decision was made to file bankruptcy to protect the hotel from the scads of creditors who kept materializing.

At the same time, I filed a lawsuit against the bank for not supervising the disbursement of construction funds as they had originally agreed to. I had to shut down my business to manage the mess and entered the hospital for the first of three surgeries over a 10-month period. I did not like life very much!

How did it all work out? Since my former partner filed for personal bankruptcy, I was left holding the creditor bag. The hotel business did grow, and would have shown a profit if it weren't for the construction loan baggage I inherited. After two years, I negotiated its sale. The bank settled the suit (those ever-present attorneys walked away with most of the money). I liquidated all my assets at fire sale prices (a loss close to one million dollars) and paid the creditors and attorneys in full.

The court, the attorneys, and the creditors considered it a successful bankruptcy. I considered it a colossal failure. I felt ruined. My business was gone, my net worth evaporated, my family's financial security eroded, my health deteriorated, my friends . . . well, I learned that some *weren't*. How could I have been so stupid to get caught in this web?

Meanwhile, as our evening and stories wound down, we promised to get together again soon. Yes, we all agreed that success was grand. But reliving our failures—thanks, but no thanks. We also noted both men and women verbally patted us on the back when successes were heralded in the print and media. But opinions about failure were different. Men accepted them; some even viewed them as a badge of courage, strength, and something to grow from. Women viewed failure as being tainted, as if one had cooties.

Failure is a Fact of Life

Successful men and women are separated from those who are not successful by their attitude about failure. People who are successful don't fear it. But they feel that failure, though they don't like it, is one of the best things that happened to them. They recognize rebirthings can happen. At some point in your life, you will experience failure. Whether it's a public or private, it happens.

Failure has stages similar to the ones identified by Elizabeth Kubler-Ross in her book *On Death and Dying*: denial, anger, bargaining, letting go, and acceptance. Carole Hyatt and Linda Gottlieb wrote *When Smart People Fail,* an international best seller. In their section on *The Anatomy of Failure*, they also identify stages of failure: shock, fear, anger, blame, shame, and despair.

According to Hyatt and Gottlieb, failure is a judgment about an event or events. Whether a failure is personal or professional, it impacts self-esteem, social status, and money. When their book was first published, they described failure as the "last taboo." It was considered by most to be embarrassing and a secret that shouldn't be discussed publicly. If you failed, you were shamed!

Since then, much has happened in the world. Big businesses have collapsed and solid employees with impeccable reputations have lost their jobs. Failure, in fact, has become a fact of life for many . . . which means it's normal. The good news—it is no longer a taboo subject. The bad news—it doesn't hurt any less.

When failure hits, it's common to feel you are alone, that only *you* are experiencing the pain, the humiliation, the financial disaster, and the status as a social outcast (whether perceived or real). If you are going through failure of some sort, you are inclined to believe it is a unique, first-time-in-the-universe's lifetime experience.

The downsizing mania of the '90s has been the door opener for acknowledging failure and thus finding the freedom to discuss it. Thousands of women and men who have done a terrific job for their companies got pink slips. The subject of failure moved from the back page of the newspapers to the front, and was routinely spoken about on radio and television news broadcasts. Still, when failure occurs, it is absolutely normal to feel the shock and the need to hide, to disappear.

Some failures are years in the making; others occur in a very short period of time. When failure is at your doorstep, it is common to feel isolated and numb, and to blame others or cite economic factors. Later, the full range of pain hits—emotional and, for some, physical. Failure happens for a variety of reasons. But most people, shortly after it hits or in the midst of it, aren't able to step back to interpret how, why, and even when it all began. It's only later that you can honestly determine what part you played. This scrutiny is critical. In *When Smart People Fail*, nine common reasons for failure are identified:

➤ Poor Interpersonal Skills
➤ The Wrong Fit
➤ The Halfhearted Effort: Lack of Commitment
➤ The Wild Card: Bad Luck
➤ Self-Destructive Behavior
➤ Too Scattered to Focus
➤ Sexism, Racism and Ageism
➤ Poor Management: Over- or Under-delegation
➤ Hanging On

See which one(s) fit you.

Poor Interpersonal Skills

This area is the primary cause of career failure, but few realize it. Hyatt says that most people blame "office politics" for failure, then adds, "Office politics are really nothing more than office interactions among people." She likens interpersonal skills to "social intelligence" which consists of five components:

> ➢ Being sensitive to others
> ➢ Being able to listen
> ➢ Giving and taking criticism
> ➢ Being emotionally steady
> ➢ Being able to build team support

Developing social intelligence provides a tremendous support mechanism when disaster hits. Your ability to give and receive criticism well—knowing how to listen and being sensitive to others—is invaluable when bad times and bad news hit you. You'll find you have a support network in place. Whether your failure is caused by outside forces (you lost your job because your position was eliminated along with a lot of others, or you simply blew it), people will be there to support you.

The Wrong Fit

When companies merged and downsized, a lot of wrong fits were created; the chemistry just didn't work. The new boss or manager wants to bring in his or her own team. It has nothing to do with what skills and loyalty you bring to the company. It's just that "you don't fit."

This is where the entrepreneurial spirit breaks out. In the '70s, I learned I was a maverick. I had my own ideas and opinions, and I often disagreed with the company's philosophy. I was the wrong fit, and eventually left to start my own company in 1977. Since then, I have been self-employed.

The Halfhearted Effort: Lack of Commitment

Lack of commitment is linked to both low self-esteem and self-confidence. If you are a "non-committer," you're less inclined to jump into things; you avoid participating in anything unless you see it as a sure thing. In the end, you set yourself up for failure. Anyone who is successful has had a steady stream of risks cross their trail to success. Without question, a failure can damage your self-esteem, and a string of them can be insurmountable. As your feeling of self-worth declines, you're less likely to stick your neck out into other ventures. In effect, low self-esteem supports, even encourages, other failures.

Many of the men and women from **The Confidence Factor** felt that, in the midst of a failure when their self-esteem was knocked down, they had to adopt an attitude of "Fake it . . . until you make it." They simply pretended their confidence was intact. No matter what the disaster was, they painted it as a mere hiccup in their career or personal paths.

It is like looking in the mirror. If you scowl, the image scowls back—not an energy inducement, to say the least. But when you smile and project confidence, the image looking back reflects the same. By faking it until you make it, those you meet on the outside respond positively, which in turn allows you to do the same. A new cycle begins.

The Wild Card: Bad Luck

Bad things happen and you can't control it. You can't stop it; you can't divert it. It just happens. If your company merges with another, brings in a new team and you're not on it, there is little you can do. In today's fast-forward, high-tech environment, it is probable that whatever the state of the art is now, it will be obsolete next year.

Can you do anything about a wild-card phenomenon? Hyatt says no. She also advises that you shouldn't blame yourself. It just happens. Let go and move on.

The Self-Destruction Behavior

Deja Vu. The broken record. The cycle repeats. You've been there before—it's the repetition of behavior that leads to some type of downfall. It could be a bad temper; it could be verbal attacks—unkind or foul language; it could be fantasizing—out of touch with reality. It could even be the giggles! Whatever the pattern is, you keep repeating it.

Giggling uncontrollably in a stressful or sensitive negotiation can significantly diminish your value to others. Being a hot head and stomping out of a meeting is job suicide. Barking at others with abusive language can eliminate any support you might have. Whatever it is, you are the mistress or master and must control your actions . . . that is, if you want to change your self-destructive behavior.

Once you have identified that you have displayed some type of behavior deemed inappropriate by others, you must make a conscious decision. Do you want to maintain that behavior, or change it? If you don't see it as a problem, it's doubtful you'll want to change. But if you do recognize it as a damper on your success or the cause of failure, you have two choices: stop it, or continue it. If you continue it, it is highly probable you will recycle failure.

Too Scattered To Focus

Anyone who is too scattered to focus has too much on his or her platter. People have limits as to how much they can accomplish. Some people are so good at keeping several balls in the air; they never let any land . . . at least not the big ones. Yet most of their work is either mediocre or never gets noticed.

There are also people who are brilliant in their accomplishments. They believe they have the Midas touch; everything they do turns to gold. Hyatt calls them "risk junkies"—people who enjoy living on the edge. When they are successful, they are Queen (or King), and believe their successes will never end. When risk junkies bomb, they fail big.

Unless you're one of those perfect people with the Midas touch, getting overextended leads to failure. The solution is to practice saying "No." You can't do it all . . . at least, not all at the same time. Concentrate on one or two areas and go with it. Success will follow.

Sexism, Ageism and Racism

The "isms"—prejudicial "isms"—are often used as excuses for failure. You may feel you've been discriminated against at work, at church, in the community because you are black, or Latino, or Asian, or female or male. It could be you just didn't do the job, but your ego gets in the way and you seek a rationalization for the outcome.

There are, though, times when the "isms" are quite valid. You may have grounds for sexual discrimination at work, for example. And when that happens, you have to make a decision. Combating the prejudice can be expensive and, in some cases, difficult to prove. If you have solid, well-documented information and the funds to finance a legal battle (or find a law firm to work on a contingency basis), then you can take your issue through the court system. If you don't have the money, the time, the documentation, or the energy, then you need to seek other solutions.

Part of any solution is assessing who and what you are, and what you want to do in your next position. If sexism is an issue, you might be better served in a smaller, more entrepreneurial type of company. Sexism is usually more blatant in larger, well-established companies . . . especially when men are the primary players in middle management and above. Racism is less tolerated in large organizations because the companies themselves are more subject to public scrutiny and there is a greater diversity in their work force.

Ageism is the fastest growing complaint filed with the federal government's Equal Employment Opportunity Commission, the EEOC. Losing a job after your mid-50s is a handicap. It's tough to compete with the "kids" who hire in for less money. Hyatt advises you to use age to your advantage. While it may be held against you in the corporate world, it's not when you are your own boss. Age means experience. Hyatt says,

> Instead of endlessly, and often futilely fighting a gray-haired battle to get back into the corporate world, why not use the opportunity created by your failure to make a real change? Take a look around your community and try to spot an opening in the service sector. What service have you always wished existed? Many have used the defeat handed them by a youth-worshipping society to discover that they are late-in-life entrepreneurs.

Poor Management: Over- or Under-Delegation

Management is an art. It's not inbred but learned over a period of time. Everyone has strengths and weaknesses, talents and non-talents. If you are outgoing, energetic, charismatic, and have been described as a visionary, you are far more likely to be placed in the entrepreneur or leadership arena.

Apple Computer's Steve Jobs is a good example of the perfect entrepreneur. He had the vision, charisma, energy, and talent to take an idea—the personal computer—and grow it. It started in a garage with his partner Steve

Wozniack, and grew into today's multi-billion-dollar, international corporation. But he couldn't carry it all the way. He was stopped in midstream because his entrepreneurial management style, or lack of it, eventually got in his way. Eventually Apple's Board of Directors brought in John Sculley to take over the reins of management. Since then, Sculley has been booted, as have several subsequent CEOs. And Jobs is back at the helm, recreating Apple once again.

Initially, Jobs had the vision, energy, and enthusiasm to carry the company to a certain level. But to take it to the next level—into the multi-billion-dollar realm—he didn't have the management skills and talent. Sometimes he couldn't let go, and at other times, he let just anyone take charge of critical projects.

The Small Business Administration estimates the maximum number of employees that entrepreneurs can manage is 40. Apple Computer employed many times that number, and Jobs found himself out of his element. He was the wrong fit at the time.

The bottom line is to recognize your strengths and weaknesses. If you are good at choosing people to work with you and for you, delegate and let them shine.

Hanging On

How many people do you know who love what they do? Probably not a lot. Some can get up each day and find that going to work is a joy. If that doesn't sound like you, most likely you know you should be looking and stretching and moving into other areas. But for some reason, you can't. You hang on; you become complacent, even apathetic.

The primary factor for hanging on, or being stuck, is the fear of change. In some ways, it is safe to stay put and have a small measure of comfort in being familiar with your position. After all, a lot of people have lost jobs, so fear crystallizes the attitude that you'd better hold on to what you've got. Hanging on is a different type of failure. Being fired or wiped out financially is easily measured— it happened. You had it then; you don't have it now. Hanging on is internal . . . and usually invisible to the outsider. Hyatt adds,

> When you feel that you can't move on, you are no longer in control, you experience negative self-talk. You end up being totally disappointed in yourself. The solution is to tell yourself, "This is only temporary; there are lots of options out there." When you can step back and explore those options, you will add to your self-esteem and build up a belief system that you can move on.

For whatever reason, failure happens, and it happens to the best of people. Rarely once, but many times. Failure is often a factor in many of the chapters in this book. The very painful stories of Charlene, Liz, Lucy, and myself were included to let you know that each of us survived. Would we want to relive those days? Are you kidding? Each of us subscribed to the poem, Don't Quit—

Don't Quit

When things go wrong as they sometimes will, when
 the road you're trudging seems all uphill,
When the funds are low and the debts are high,
 and you want to smile but you have to sigh,
When care is pressing you down a bit—rest if
 you must, *but don't you quit.*

For life is queer with its twists and turns, as every
 one of us sometimes learns.
And many a person turns about, when she might
 have won had she stuck it out.
Don't give up though the pace seems slow, you may
 succeed with another blow.

Often the goal is nearer than it seems to the faint
 and struggling heart;
Often the struggler has given up, when he might
 have captured the victor's cup—
And he learned too late when night came down,
 how close he was to the golden crown.

Success is failure turned inside out—the silver tint
 of the clouds of doubt.
And you never can tell how close you are, it
 may be near when it seems afar.
So stick to the fight when you're hardest hit,
 it's when things seem worst that *you must not quit.*
       —Anonymous

If you are presently experiencing failure, ask yourself—
what will this failure do to you? Will it destroy you personally? Will it destroy your family? Will it destroy your
job? Most likely, the answer will be "no" to all three.

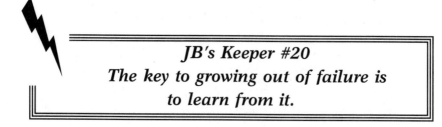

JB's Keeper #20
The key to growing out of failure is
to learn from it.

Chapter Nineteen

 Loyalty—The Job
Doesn't Love You

Loyalty can be blinding. You love your job and you love your employer—you are loyal. Yet an employer professes love for the employees only when the bottom-line profit picture is satisfactory—the company is loyal, but its "love" is conditional.

Many loyal employees have had to face the harsh reality of that fickle love. Some people fully understand the recent business trends of acquisitions, mergers, consolidation, profit taking, overfunded pension plans, and so on. But you don't need a high-level degree to understand that none of these trends have you, the employee, in mind. It's money, not you, that commands the ultimate loyalty of many employers today.

A business that's here today may be gone tomorrow and the reason behind its disappearance may not always be as simple as bankruptcy. If you were working for a company that was changing direction or experiencing financial problems, what would you do?

A. Hang in there, hoping it would get better.
B. Volunteer to work longer hours until it turns around.
C. Offer to take a cut in pay.
D. Update your resume and circulate it.

Many women would automatically answer A, B or C (possibly all three). A man would most likely answer D, then hedge with a little bit of A—hoping he has a new job to go to before the doors close. Women are more likely to hang on to their present position, even when job security is at an all time low. They continue to believe these *Momisms*: "They need me," "I'm the only one that knows where everything is," "I can't desert them when everyone else is leaving them," or "I love my job." All these emotional responses don't include a shred of the logic needed in today's volatile employment situations. Men decide that they want off the ship before it sinks.

Okay, so you feel emotionally attached to your job. Think rationally now. Does *it* really love you? Does *it* call you when you are blue and need an encouraging word? Does *it* bring you a cup of tea when you don't feel well? Does *it* share an intimate story with you? Does *it* make you laugh? Does *it* wipe your tears or give you a hug at just the right moment? Does *it* tell you are wonderful, even when you don't feel wonderful? Does *it* tell you that you look terrific, even when you have a "bad hair" day? The answer is No. Individuals at work may do those things. But the company itself is like the Tin Man from the Wizard of Oz; it has no heart. And, sadly, it isn't even looking for one.

When things sour in the workplace, it is easy to rationalize why someone adopts a "hands off" or "let it be" posture, choosing the status quo rather than seeking a new situation. The two primary reasons are fear and denial. That includes fear of change itself and fear of not being able to get another job. Denial means not believing change could have a negative impact. But if you stay loyal to your fickle company, and live with that fear and denial for a period of time, what happens to you as a person? Certainly, your fears will come true. It's best to face the changes rationally and look for new employment.

Not My Department. . .Not Me

Before being "forced" into retirement, Jack was a professor and chair of the science and engineering departments in a small East Coast college. His chairmanship had been awarded after several years of proving himself. He had single handedly upgraded his science department—both the faculty and course design. Upon his arrival, he found much of the equipment was outdated and unsuitable for its present use—in fact, it bordered on being dangerous to faculty and students.

The college offered a degree program in computer science, yet the school wasn't even computerized. Jack took it on himself to obtain grants and gifts of computers from one of the giants in the industry. It was natural for him to feel that being part of the team meant using his expertise in fund raising so the college could be part in the modern technological world.

For eight years, his contributions in upgrading and expanding his departments outweighed, by far, those of any other department chair. He believed it was critical for the school to be more competitive with the prestigious universities in the region. And it would be a feather in his cap that he had spearheaded the advancement in the curriculum.

Despite his efforts, all was not well at the college. Enrollment was down somewhat and the well-liked Dean of the Business School departed. His resignation created a hole in the leadership of the college and, for Jack, the loss of an ally. Shortly after this resignation, a meeting of all department chairs was called. He was caught totally off guard when the Dean (Letters and Sciences) told him all engineering classes would be eliminated immediately and his position would be phased out in a year.

Jack's years of hard work—work that was rarely recognized let alone paid for—seemed to have no value to the college. He had been rendered invisible. Even then, during his final year on the faculty, he spent extra hours creating new classes and experiments for his science students. But what he *didn't* do was put effort into finding another position. At 57, he found himself prematurely retired, a duck out of water. With his high level of education, he was too expensive and too old for another institution to consider hiring. He remembered the situation this way,

> I allowed my personal drive to cloud the truth that the college was headed in a direction different from the one what I was working on. I wasn't a member of the "ruling elite"—Deans and above; their vision for the future didn't include mine. This was so hard for me. I loved my job and the work I did.
>
> When Ron (the Dean of the Business School) took a position with a university in another state, I felt abandoned. I lived in denial during the two years that the school was shifting its emphasis. When I was told by my Dean that all engineering classes would be eliminated, I couldn't believe it. All my work would be trashed. Still, I kept telling myself I

was important and the school needed my creativity and work.

I was sure that they (the Board of Directors and various Deans) would change their minds. I had been incredibly loyal. I believed they would realize what was the right thing to do. They didn't. I became one of many faculty members phased out over a two-year period.

Jack practiced what so many have. Loyalty. Too much of it. Hanging on until the end. Then, it's too late to land easily on both feet. Emotion instead of logic prevailed; self-esteem was lost and a feeling of trust violated.

Assessing Your Job

Let's determine your own attitude to your job. Use the following quiz to determine if you are ready to change jobs, want to change jobs, or may be forced to change jobs. Answer a, b, or c for each question.

Quiz: Is Your Job the Right Fit?

1. **The author of *1001 Ways To Leave Your Job* is speaking and signing his book at your local book store.** You would:
   a) Go and buy several copies of the book for your three daughters who are discontent with their jobs.
   b) Worry that your boss will be suspicious if she overhears you making plans to go to the lecture.
   c) Attend the lecture and ask the author for his recommendations on other sources for preparing a resume or writing a business plan for self-employment.

2. **You've just won the 20-million-dollar lottery.**
   You would:
   a) Enroll in a class on painting in watercolors, start gathering brochures on Seminars Abroad with the Masters, host a ritzy dinner at the most expensive place in town, tell your family that it is "Disney World or Bust," and take a year off.
   b) Pay off your mortgage and all your credit card debt, place money aside for your grandchildren's' college education, and enroll in a class on investment strategies.
   c) Rent office space downtown, give immediate notice at your job, and announce to anyone within earshot you are starting your own business.

3. **Your best friend has sold her company.** At the celebration dinner, you:
   a) Express your excitement and tell her you are thrilled she will have more time for her friends.
   b) Wish that you two could start your own company, sell it someday, and make a fortune.
   c) Wish you had owned stock in her company to cash in when she cashed out.

4. **Your spouse has been laid off and decides to return to school full time.** You:
   a) Feel it is good to have at least one parent home at different times throughout the day. Being a student allows for that.
   b) Realize that your job doesn't deliver the cash flow your family needs. You must start hunting for a second job.
   c) Think he is lucky and wish you could go back to school, too.

5. **After a two-week vacation, you return to the office and are overwhelmed by the amount of work on your desk.** You:
   a) Plan on leaving early, claiming you need to go to another function.
   b) Dread listening to your voice mail and avoid turning on your computer to see how much e-mail you received.
   c) Realize how much you hate your job.

6. **Your company is planning its annual retreat with you as one of the key presenters.** You:
   a) Plan on taking a few extra vacation days and ask your spouse to come up for a special weekend for two.
   b) Plan on getting the flu, forcing you to cancel out.
   c) Write the presentation and give a copy of the disk to your boss for safekeeping.

7. **You just received the announcement of your high school's ten-year reunion.** You:
   a) Buy a dress one size smaller than you are now and go on a diet.
   b) Worry that you can't take the extra time off to "schmooze" with your old friends.
   c) Wish you could be returning to the reunion as a founder of a multi-billion-dollar computer company, which owns a summer retreat in the Hamptons.

8. **You haven't taken a day off in two years.** You feel:
   a) That you are accumulating time for a good cause (your family) and will take the summer off in five years.

    b) Grateful to not have been laid off and are scared to take any time off.

    c) Angry that you don't (or can't) take time off.

9. **Rumors are circulating that a massive layoff at your company is coming.** Do you:
   a) Figure out your accumulated vacation days and plan a holiday with your family.
   b) Immediately get your resume updated, send it out, and contact a headhunter that specializes in your area.
   c) Make an appointment with your boss to discuss a possible settlement or severance package.

10. **If you could change what you'd be doing five years from today,** it would be:
   a) Only working three to four days a week and participating more in family activities.
   b) Working at the same thing you are doing now but doing it for more money.
   c) Not what you are presently doing.

How to score:

✓ If you have more A answers, you may need to prioritize and spend more time with yourself, you family, and friends.

✓ If you have more B answers, update your resume and start your job search before management tells you to.

✓ If you have more C answers, begin to take action to change careers or even start your own business.

What's Hot Today May Be Cool Tomorrow

Any type of career change made in the last few years will be dramatically different from the routine processes used in the '80s and early '90s. This is due in part to economic, technological, and political changes—as well as an expanded numbers of men and women looking for positions.

I moved to Denver, Colorado, in December of 1990. Shortly after I moved, dramatic reductions of personnel through layoffs and offers of early retirement have been generated by the Colorado "biggies." US West (now Qwest), Gates Rubber Co., Samsonite, Xcel Energy, Lucent Technologies and others have eliminated thousands of positions. Ten years ago, these companies were known as sure and safe bets; you could start your career with one of them and expect to retire comfortably on their pension plans.

What happened? Big corporations revamped their priorities. They learned that growth isn't the only way to increase profitability; they could cut overhead. This meant a lot of regional headquarters were closed and operations consolidated into other cities. The resulting employee cuts were and still are heaviest in middle management.

Those employees who stayed too long suffered the worst, despite the fact the signs were fairly easy to read—cutbacks, freezes in pay and hiring, negative articles in the media that noted decreased earnings or large write-offs. There was always a "but" or a "maybe" in the minds of the timid ones—and in the end, staying was so much easier than changing. By the time these employees left (or the position was eliminated or the doors closed), other job opportunities had vanished. Their hesitancy to change and their misplaced loyalty took them down the wrong path.

On the flip side, other companies boomed. Most were led by entrepreneurs who saw new opportunities, such as subcontracting services to larger companies who had downsized. Most small companies don't offer the cafeteria menu of perks and benefits that had been traditional practice with "big" companies.

Nor do they hire employees who had made themselves marketable with new skills and showed enthusiasm in their new employer's vision for growth. As a rule, these employees received pay rates lower than what they had received in the past. The trade off came in feeling a revitalized energy and excitement in the workplace compared with negativity and fear of the past. And—thankfully—they had jobs.

Pat worked in a busy association that offered a myriad of services to its members. The for-profit association was owned by a large Japanese conglomerate looking to sell it. When the winds of change at the top management level started to blow, he started to get antsy. He had been a major contributor to the growth of the association for the past four years, and his marketing communications work was highly praised and appreciated. Yet he felt uncomfortable with how the new leaders were treating employees.

His first impulse was to quit, but that would be an impractical move financially. So he cast around for job leads in his community, and landed a position as a writer for a small Web site development company. The owner/entrepreneur, in fact, had been a professional associate for a number of years. Working in this growing, innovative company with only seven employees proved to be a smart career move. Meanwhile, those co-workers who stayed at the association were told two months after Pat left that the operation had been sold. The new owners decided to close the doors. Forty people lost their jobs, but Pat wasn't among the casualties. He saw the winds of change coming and did something before they turned into a hurricane.

What's Hot and Not So Hot

Each year, magazines such as *Working Woman, Business Week, Fast Company, Fortune, Forbes, Inc.,* etc. all do various articles on where the action is in the job market. With a few taps, the Internet opens up incredible possibilities. On-line resume services are multi—each linked with others that opens up a whole new world of career options.

What's hot includes:

Technology and Internet Companies
Just about anything in technology, biotechnology, and the Internet is hot. If your not already a subscriber to *Fast Company, B:B2000* or some of the other newer magazines that tell all from what's what and who's who in the Internet game, start your subscriptions today.

Companies like Cisco Systems, Microsoft, Oracle, Amazon.com and AOL-Time Warner will not be going out of business in the foreseeable future. There are thousands of Internet and technology related companies that offer the sky is the limit possibilities. Annual salary ranges for these companies start in the low $20,000s a year and range to $65,000 plus.

Software Programmer
Programmers are the tech age translators—the computer language experts. Their work with computer language codes translates text, video, and sound into computer software that responds when you hit the right key(s) on your computer keyboard. Some of these highly skilled "hotshots" take existing data base software and customize it for a single business customer—a real need for those who hate learning from computer manuals. Annual salaries range from $28,000 to $70,000 and up. With

technology changing on a daily basis, anyone who has a programming talent is very employable.

Advanced Practice Nurse

When nurses go back to school and get training and skills in other areas such as nurse practitioner, nurse midwifery or nurse-anesthetist, they can substantially increase their income. Salaries range from $43,000 to $100,000 annually.

Employee Assistance Program Counselor

One of the hottest fields in Human Resources is the EAP Counselor who works with employees referred by their company for intervention in substance abuse and mental health problems. Salary ranges from $42,000 to $60,000 a year.

Bank Financial Services Marketer

Most banks have established separate investment services and hire commission only or salary plus commission reps. They sell in-house mutual funds and other investment products. Salaries can range widely: $25,000 a year for a sales assistant to $110,000 for a sales manager.

Destination Marketer

As a marketer, your job is to "sell" your city to potential meeting planners who will bring a convention into town. Depending on the job within the company, salaries can range from $20,000 to more than $100,000 a year.

The Information Highway leads the pack for top jobs. Opportunities abound in network systems, services, or systems operations. As technology expands, so will the range of jobs. Most new jobs will come from service sectors; the majority of these new positions haven't been created yet. Your challenge is to have your antenna up and tune in to opportunities as they open up.

The bottom line is that change is everywhere. The only role misplaced loyalty plays is in stifling your progress. Over-staying in a job can be likened to moving deck chairs around on the Titanic. It's important to be realistic and rational, and not overly emotional, when it comes to building your career.

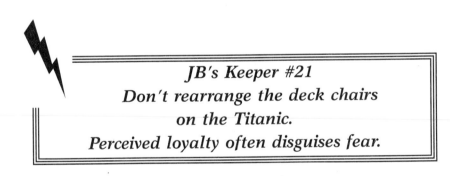

JB's Keeper #21
Don't rearrange the deck chairs
on the Titanic.
Perceived loyalty often disguises fear.

Chapter Twenty

Negotiating—
Not for Kids Only

Are you a parent? Or do you have friends or relatives with young children? If you answered "yes" to either question, you have no doubt experienced the true masters of negotiating: kids. Kids from the age of two and up know how to negotiate with adults. They also know what buttons to push to get your attention, and they know what look or smile will melt your heart. They quickly learn which gestures and looks of yours they can "milk" . . . and which ones to avoid.

Somehow, what you learned by intuition as a child, you forgot as you matured into the adult world. What a shame to have to relearn tools that were so much a part of you when you were very young! Every day you will enter into some type of negotiation . . . determining with your sister who will host the family party, negotiating with your spouse where to go for vacation, making agreements with your kids on getting chores done, coming to a final price with a salesman. It could be as simple as determining a meeting place or as intense as negotiating to stay alive.

Staying alive? For many, negotiating is equivalent to conflict and therefore should be avoided. To some, it's almost life threatening. But listen and realize this—*learning how to negotiate will resolve conflict, not create it.*

The 80/20 Solution

Viewing negotiation as a matter of cooperation and problem resolution rather than one of conflict creation is the first step in establishing a negotiating mentality. Negotiation plays a key role in your workplace and personal life. But first and foremost, get prepared; in any negotiation, 80 percent involves planning and only 20 percent is action.

Being prepared means knowing what you want, and knowing what the other side wants. In any bargaining process, be sure to have a clear picture of your goal. If you don't have that in mind, the outcome could be significantly different from what you desire.

When you negotiate, you always hope for the best but would be wise to *plan for the worst!* Rehearse your spiel and anticipate the critical points by giving good answers. Set the stage; assemble the right people at the right place at the right time. Have a game plan in mind; establish ground rules for the process to help everyone focus on the end result. But realize that, despite all your preparations, sometimes even the best-laid plans go awry. You could be faced with an impasse—and find out your desires may not be fully satisfied. When that's the case, one of the strongest strategies of negotiation is to walk away.

Keep It Clear

Negotiation is the give-and-take, back-and-forth process of solving problems, large and small, that arise every day while you try to obtain or accomplish something. The essence of any good negotiation is clear communication. You will be ahead of the game if you recognize that everyone has a different communication style. Determine what style(s) will come into play before a negotiation begins. According to Nicole Schapiro, author of *Negotiating For Your Life* and *The Dance of Negotiation*, negotiation is done on many levels, from simple bartering to problem solving and conflict resolution.

Cooperative negotiation achieves a balance between two differing points of views—what Schapiro calls "partnership negotiation." It's a mutual education process. Partnership negotiation eliminates "ego exchange negotiation"—a negotiation that is only used to put on a display of power and pretense. She observes that many negotiations get off on the wrong foot because one or both sides are insensitive to differing cultural factors.

A partnership negotiation absolutely requires awareness of the personal and situational variables inherent in multi-cultural relationships—business, professional, and interpersonal dealings along with casual contacts in everyday living and travel. Implicit mutual respect for one another's value system is a basis for initial trust in any dialogue. Without that respect, making a deal is virtually impossible.

Know Exactly What You Want

It's important that you set goals. Knowing what you want or need to come away with is a strong card in your negotiation hand. If it is a materialistic goal, name it and quantify it; if it is something intangible, describe it sufficiently to give it some substance. Here's a surprise in negotiating: others are often more willing to give you what you want if they know *exactly* what you want. Don't waste a good opportunity to negotiate by displaying a confrontational expression of your general dissatisfaction. You won't have a chance of getting what you want from a person who feels attacked or unduly criticized.

Reach high. If you don't set your aspirations high, you won't get the "best" deal. You probably won't get the worst either. In retrospect, you may be disappointed. It's rare that anyone gets more than what they ask for. Most women set far too modest goals when they negotiate for money or position. Don't join the crowd. Visualize the best possible scenario and you just may get it. In simple terms, don't sell yourself short.

Believe it or not, claiming authority over your own life is critical in preparing to negotiate for your life—and that authority is a non-negotiable requirement. Schapiro's wise words include this advice,

> You cannot trade off the right to make decisions
> about your life for money, love, security, prestige,
> affection or fame—and not until you reclaim yourself,
> or understand what you are about, will you be able
> to go forward.
> Don't confuse "authority" with "control." The
> desire to have total control over your life is
> unrealistic since you may depend upon others also.
> You cannot control the behavior of other people—in
> your own families or in the world—and you can't
> control the course of nature. Within that reality, it's
> foolish to think that you, who functions every
> moment of your life in conversation with other

people in the natural world around you, can be in total control.

However, you can have authority over your life. You can choose to be the final decision-maker on important issues that concern your minds, your bodies, and your work.

What's Not Negotiable

Some areas of your life are non-negotiable. That includes age—you can't change it. But you can do a number of things to minimize its negative influence by taking care of your health. Practice preventive health measures such as adequate exercise, proper diet, and regular check-ups. It's also impossible to change your genetic heritage or parentage. So make yourself and any birth children you have aware of the inherent strengths and weaknesses of these factors. That's how you can capitalize on and also minimize the effects of these non-negotiables.

A physical handicap can be an additional factor to contend with. You can't negotiate for better eyesight or hearing. A paralyzed limb or a learning disability is a fact of life for some. If you are disabled, however, you may be able to negotiate for better circumstances that allow you to perform effectively both at home and at work.

Disease can also be a part of life. Unfortunately, the outcome of some diseases are, today, non-negotiable. We all hope that medical science will offer some negotiating power to combat cancer, Alzheimer's, diabetes, AIDs, and a labyrinth of other diseases. But that doesn't mean all your treatment choices are taken away. If you or someone you know is seriously ill, be conscious of your role in determining an appropriate type of treatment and selecting who will administer it.

The Do's and Don'ts

I have known Nicole Schapiro since the early '80s. This gem she gave me has assisted me countless times: At the beginning of any negotiation, don't fuss over your first sentence. It's usually a throwaway and no one pays attention to it. Make it casual, humorous, and welcoming. But the next sentence is crucial. Address the second sentence to the person who has the real power.

Concerning the setting for your negotiation, determining where you sit should be very strategic. If you are aware that an individual you know will disagree with any solution you propose, sit next to him or her. You will then appear confident and brave in your ability to handle pressure at such close proximity. If this naysayer is someone you don't know, it's more appropriate to sit across from him or her so you can establish eye contact and observe body language. This allows you to get a handle on the other person's personality and conflict style as well as his or her intentions. Negotiation "Do's and Don'ts" include the following:

- *Don't* go in cold. You can't wing it.
- *Do* bring in some facts that you prepared in advance.

- *Don't* pitch to the wrong person, someone who can't do anything for you.
- *Do* see the decision-maker.

- *Don't* force your style on someone by giving reams of paper to a bottom-liner, or handing one piece of paper to someone whom only acts on reams of information.
- *Do* be aware of the person's personality and work style; try to match it.

- *Don't* become overly emotional.
- *Do* stay calm and focused on your goal. Ask what is the goal and what are the obstacles.

- *Don't* assume anything.
- *Do* know what you *do* know, and what you *don't* know.

- *Don't* argue or attack.
- *Do* be willing to make concessions without forfeiting your goal.

If you are feeling besieged with personal and/or professional disappointments—if you feel needy or just scared—stop the negotiation process. Entering into a negotiation during these times is not in your best interest. If you are under the pressure of a deadline and don't have the luxury of sufficient time to complete a negotiation, go back to Chapter 2 on Confidence: Who Needs It? Reread and process through *The 10 Steps to Building Confidence* as a booster. Pay particular attention to Step 2: Delete Negativity—Being Positive Isn't a Myth; Step 6: You're Never Alone—Going Solo Is for Sissies; Step 7: Expect the Unexpected—It's Life; and Step 8: Create Bravos—Take Your Credit.

To be successful, become committed to learning the negotiation process well. Tell yourself you are a great negotiator. Most people assume they aren't—so be different. Your attitude, though, is just the beginning.

When you enter any negotiation, make use of the body language of the parties involved—yours and theirs—to your advantage. Here are a few tips to identifying when a person is resistant to, or cooperating with, the negotiating process.

Resistant Body Language:
➤ Eye contact is non-existent.
➤ Desk tapping or pounding occurs.
➤ Hands are clenched into fists (with or without pounding).
➤ Body movements are nervous—fidgeting, knee swinging, foot tapping.
➤ Body is stiffly upright, with leg and/or arms tightly crossed.
➤ Eyes shift repetitively to a door or window.

When these things are occurring, your negotiating challenge is much greater. Stick more firmly than ever with your tactics. You might even ask if something else is on that person's mind and work to eliminate any obstacles such as taking a break to make an urgent phone call. If it seems appropriate, ask to reschedule to a time when he or she can be more receptive.

Cooperative Body Language:
➤ Continuous eye contact is made with the speaker.
➤ Body leans forward toward the speaker.
➤ Legs and arms are relaxed, not crossed.
➤ Head is tilted toward the speaker in a listening position.
➤ Head nods affirmatively.

When you see these indicators of a cooperative attitude, your negotiations are more likely to go smoothly.

Important Factors
Whenever you contemplate a negotiation of any type, first get the facts. Being prepared puts you ahead of the game. Your preparation will identify your goals, the areas in which you are open to compromise (if any), and the amount of time you will commit to the process. During

the negotiations, listen carefully and speak clearly. All are vital factors.

As you practice negotiating, you will have some successes getting what you want along the way. And, as your skills build through the use and exchange of ideas, it will become crystal clear why the art of negotiation is a critical tool for survival today. Through negotiation, you will get far more of what you want . . . and far less of what you don't want.

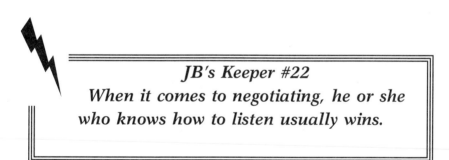

JB's Keeper #22
When it comes to negotiating, he or she who knows how to listen usually wins.

Chapter Twenty-One

 Change—Learn to Become
a Shift Shaper

According to futurist and trend forecaster Faith Popcorn, change is here to stay. Not only that, the rate of change will continue to increase. Society changed as much in the decade of the '90s as it did from 1940 through 1990.

In the five years between 2000 to 2005, society will experience the equivalent of another 50 years of change! Popcorn tells us if we live through the next 15 years, we will actually live through 100 years of change . . . or the equivalent of what the decades of 1940 to 1990 delivered. Here's how that looks:

    1940–1990 = 50 years of change
    1990–2000 = 50 years of change
    2000–2005 = 50 years of change

Change is inevitable. Without it, nothing could exist, and life as present generations currently know it will disappear. For example, people over 30 years of age knows that microwaves and VCRs did not exist during their childhood, but they're commonplace now.

Think about all the now-common items invented since 1940 . . . the personal computer, penicillin, the Pill, artificial hearts, organ transplants, radar, television, FM radios, credit cards, frozen foods, pantyhose, and ball point pens. And these only scratch the surface! Can you imagine today's society without any of them? *FutureShock* author Alvin Toffler wrote, "Change is a process by which the future invades our lives." How true that has become.

From Non-Shifting to Shift Shaper

In 1981, I published my first book, *The Woman's Guide to Financial Savvy*. Because I thought it would be the only book that I would ever produce, I really didn't pay much attention to the process. After all, why bother when it's a one-time shot. Well, the one-time shot turned into multi-books with no end in sight today. *Stop Stabbing Yourself in the Back* is my twenty-second book. And the process that takes any work to publication has changed significantly since 1981.

I started to tune into the changes in the book business when I began work on my second book, *Money Phases*. New technology was rapidly coming on the scene. In 1979, when my agent sent the manuscript of *The Woman's Guide to Financial Savvy* to publishers, the concept of word processing was unheard of by most. It would be a few years before the computers made by the upstart kid—Apple—broke into the headlines and the workplace.

When I started to work on the second book in 1982, I heard about these new "gadgets" that were replacing the typewriter. I resisted trying one—the computer—because it wasn't cheap. Contrary to popular belief, most authors don't make a lot of money—the average income from selling books is less than $10,000 a year. I reasoned that a new computer would never pay for itself.

After all, my typewriter was good enough. And mine was impressive for its time. It had the capability of remembering 50 pages of material. In the early '80s, it was IBM's state-of-the art for small businesses. Granted, they were not used for writing books at that time. They were primarily for storing letters to be sent to my clients.

In the old days, from 1979 to 1986, I wrote my articles and books on a typewriter and retyped each page as changes were made. I recognized there must be a better way. So I persevered through five stages of change before finally accepting this new "gadget." The stages are explained below.

The Five Stages of Change

When you are faced with the change process, you experience multiple stages. They include:

1. *Resistance*—being stubborn; denying the benefits and need of an item, process or concept
2. *Skepticism*—willing to try, but still doubting the benefit and use of an item, process, or concept; clinging to the past
3. *Adaptation*—moving past reluctance and fully accepting that the item, process, or concept can be integrated into your personal or professional life
4. *Shifting*—opening up to "what if" scenarios; your transition from being stubborn to *shift shaper* is almost complete
5. *Cohesiveness*—the ways of the past are in the past; your new attitude becomes, "Why didn't I do this sooner" or "What took me so long to change?" You

have become a *shift shaper*—and you can't understand why others are still resisting change.

Will Rogers said, "Even if you're on the right track, you'll get run over if you just sit there." Wise words for today's quick changing techno world.

Shifting to New Technology

While in the process of producing book number two, I experienced the first two stages: resistance and great skepticism. I knew there was another way to do it, but believed that the old way—the typewriter—was good enough. And I wasn't convinced the new equipment could speed up a writer's work. And, I had just put out $3500 for IBM's model.

Yet, it only takes an author a short time to seek a better way than rewriting an entire manuscript, every time a paragraph needs to be moved or a few more typos are uncovered. In fact, back in the Stone Age of the '80s, it was quite common to turn in manuscripts with typos and crossed out sentences and paragraphs. We authors knew the publisher's typesetter would "clean it up." Today, clean manuscripts from author to publisher are the rule!

After some coaxing, we decided to rent a computer for a month . . . just to give it a trial run. While Louie, my secretary, embraced the genius of it, I still *resisted*. I was both *skeptical* and *hesitant*, still viewing it as a new-fangled device. But, since Louie was the one transferring my spoken words to paper, I let her have her way. It soon became obvious that the computer enhanced her speed and efficiency levels significantly.

I then moved into the third stage of change—*adaptation*. My attitude became, "Well, we'll keep it, but we won't get rid of the typewriters—we had three. After all, we could always use a typewriter if we needed to do something in a hurry. I certainly didn't know how to operate this new gadget. To me, "booting up" was what a woman did with her winter footwear. I didn't have a clue that it meant turning on the computer and opening a file.

In 1986, Louie went on a well-earned holiday and left me with written and detailed instructions on how to turn on the computer and access files I might need during her absence. At that time, I had begun research for the book that was published the following year, *Woman to Woman,* and was also working on my doctorate degree.

My agent had asked me to make a few changes in the book proposal and return a clean copy to him in New York. The change seemed simple—converting some single-spaced text to double spacing. So, tapping into the magic of technology, I booted-up the computer, opened the appropriate file, and proceeded to give it the commands to change from single to double spacing using Louie's instructions. But in the process, I deleted the entire manuscript! To say that this was not a good day for me is an understatement!

For three days, the techie experts tried to retrieve the lost material—and were unsuccessful. My emotions ran the gamut—from disbelief, to denial, then anger. Because of Louie's absence, I had no choice but to do it over—on a computer! I sat down and recreated what had been lost. What do you know? I really liked using the marvelous new gadget. The computer had the ability to erase, delete, edit, and move phrases, sentences, and paragraphs around with a tap of a key. It was unbelievable to me; my "gadget," was a writer's dream.

By the end of the day, I went from *adaptation* to the fourth stage, *shifting*. I began to wonder what else could I do with the computer and word processing programs.

What kind of overhead pages for workshops could it produce? What about creating cartoons to use during lectures? How about pasting graphs into articles? I was sold. In a nano-second, the fifth stage called *cohesiveness* hit. Within the year, five Apple Macintoshes found new homes in my office.

I was hooked, almost becoming evangelistic is my pronouncements of what my "Macs" could do. Today, 20 years later, I am still in awe of these machines. And in the process, I had become a *shift shaper* for anyone who was contemplating a computer for home or office use.

Today, I openly and loudly say I couldn't *imagine* not using a computer. I could not produce the volume of written material I do if these machines weren't an integral part of my office team. Those original three Apples have been upgraded, replaced, and added to. What happened to our state-of-the-art $3,500 IBM Memory Typewriter? I gave it away!

Resisting Resistance

Some people take forever to move beyond *resistance*. They will do whatever they can to ward off changes when the only reality is change. Cynthia was in a disappointing marriage that had lost its luster and sense of fun. Her husband rarely wanted to socialize and when they did, she felt she always had to plan around his tastes. She resisted doing anything, though, because she just didn't want to rock the boat. But her husband surprised her. He filed divorce papers and she froze in disbelief.

She honestly couldn't see her life being any better as a divorcee and viewed the possibility with such skepticism that it prevented her from preparing a response to the filing for a long time.

Thankfully, she confided in friends who cared about her

enough to convince her to take action. They recommended a divorce lawyer who helped Cynthia work through all the details. Once the legalities were taken care of, she went through the adaptation stage . . . and began to enjoy the transition of being on her own.

By this time, she had shifted her stubborn position to one of looking at life in a new way. What if she joined a dance club and learned the tango? What if she started taking piano lessons again and began to share her music with others? These ideas got her excited!

Cynthia moved into the cohesiveness stage when she recognized how much fun it was to truly enjoy the freedom of making decisions independently. She had successfully worked through the five stages of change, and could say she was having much more fun than when she was married.

In working through to the fourth stage, *shifting*, many still feel uneasy or uncomfortable. Sometimes the "good old days" seem simpler. They may be, but know that we can't turn back, we can only go forward.

When people arrive at the final stage of *cohesiveness*, they've accepted the change and can work with it comfortably, whatever "it" is. They think back and fail to remember what it was really like before the change . . . with a greater sense of confidence and control.

The Way of the VCR

Usually, people react to change in one of three ways: *reactive*, *non-active*, and *proactive*. Think of these actions as if people were VCRs. Those who are *reactive* jump out of the way, as if a car suddenly crossed the path. . They would push the "pause" button on the VCR. They'd rather not get involved. Uncertainty or lack of confidence tells them they'd be safer to step aside and see what evolves. In time, they may find that the change was exactly what they wanted, but they are too late to get on the bandwagon. They sat on the "pause" button too long.

People who are *non-active* stand still. They are paralyzed. They would push the "stop" button on the VCR. In some cases when they just want to back-peddle, they act as if they pushed the "rewind" button. Simply put, the non-active reaction means they are stuck. While in this state, it is easy to be run over, ignored, or viewed as invisible.

People who take a *proactive* position in life, however, will most likely win the race. They set the VCR at "play." They don't spend much time pausing or stopping; they get involved, ask questions, create their own future, and have a blast doing it.

Consider how you operate the VCR of your life when it comes to change. Do you push "pause", "stop" or "play"? Just realize that, if you choose to be proactive about change, you will adapt to new situations more quickly . . . and with a lot less stress.

Becoming A Shift Shaper

As a speaker, trainer, and consultant, I often find myself in the healthcare industry. This industry has undergone immense change during the past five years . . . change that will continue for several years to come. In my workshops, I sometimes ask the participants to list the areas of change that they have experienced or observed.

Some create an incredible list; others appear or act brain dead. "What change?" they ask. If "What change?" is your mantra, guaranteed, your tenure will indeed be short. You might as well write your termination notice today. Change is not invisible—it's everywhere.

Surviving and growing in a changing environment—whether it's personal or professional—takes a commitment from you. For most people, the old saying, "One for the money, two for the show, three to get ready . . . ," is never completed with the final phase "four to go." Most get stuck on getting ready; few are stuck once started. If these people operated like a VCR, they would be perpetually stay on "stop". Rarely does change not wait until you are ready to deal with it. It just happens, and moves along quickly, causing others to reach for the "pause" button. The sooner you acknowledge change and get on board, the sooner you press "play" and become a player.

While simply acknowledging the presence of change is not exactly proactive, anticipating the parameters of future change is very proactive. Begin your productive co-existence with change by making a commitment for ongoing self-improvement. Learn new things. Embrace a personal program that either enhances your current skills or expands them sufficiently to take you into another field.

Try It 21 Times and Other Tools for Change

Studies have shown that to learn new behavior, an activity needs to be reinforced approximately 21 times. One of my favorite cartoon characters is *Cathy*, created by Cathy Guisewite. In one of the strips, Cathy has embarked on a new exercise program. She gleefully proclaims to the reader that it will only take 21 days of repetition to get in the swing of the new habit. After 21 days, she will be a changed woman. But by the end of the strip, she's asking herself "What is 21 days?" Her answer: "It is 20 days, 23 hours and 59 minutes longer than the time needed to get uncomfortable with a bad habit."

Few enthusiastically jump in and wallow in change. Habits, be they bad or good, are difficult to break. Most people believe that shifting gears is scary business. Fear factors rise with change. Denial matches the level of that fear and it's easy to become paralyzed. Here are some tools to help you cope with fear and uncertainty that comes from change:

➤ Find a place and time to relax, by yourself. Breathe. Meditate. Stretch.

➤ Take walks in your neighborhood frequently. Better yet, find out where Nature Trails and Open Space Parks are located in your community. Try exploring a new trail every time you go out.

➤ Eat a balanced diet and include foods that add nutrients, not take them away (like coffee and alcohol do).

➤ Get plenty of sleep. Soak in a hot bath or get a massage before bedtime to soothe your nerves. A good sleep is the greatest source to give you energy for dealing with change.

➤ Join a support group or take a class that interests you. These activities can create a regular structure of activities that provide a sense of stability as change rages around you.

➤ Learn how to vent in healthy ways. Take time to express your emotions freely with your spouse, your friends, and a counselor. You might even turn to journal writing where you can be especially free to say what you feel.

➤ Work out faithfully at a gym or swimming pool or on your bicycle. Releasing stress during exercise gives you more energy when you have to deal with a changing situation.

➤ Create a special ritual for yourself . . . use a special place where you go regularly . . . a sanctuary . . . an activity you look forward to every day. Some choose reading; some time with "no noise"; some even choose a special show to watch; some want a little excitement where others want total calm. Whatever it is, it becomes your reward.

Whether change is forced on you or not, draw on your own courage and confidence. You will need it. Many types of jobs have been and will be eliminated as you read this. Windows close, but new doors open. Thousands—yes, even millions—of new products, opportunities, services, jobs and/or companies are created because of change.

Embracing change and being a *shift shaper* enables you to take advantage of any opportunity that may catch your eye—opportunities you had not previously envisioned or contemplated. In other words, you won't be left behind. Get ready for change.

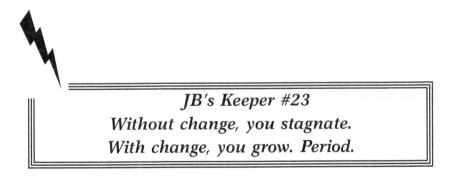

JB's Keeper #23
Without change, you stagnate.
With change, you grow. Period.

Chapter Twenty-Two

 Spirituality—
Tap Into Support from Above

Awesome. Incredibly awesome, was the reaction my husband and I shared as we sat in Faneuil Hall in Boston a cold windy October afternoon. The day before, I had participated in a television program on gender differences at the University of Massachusetts Law School. After the program, we had a pleasant lunch with the law school faculty, then looked forward to a weekend of being tourists in a city steeped with history.

I had always wanted to follow the Freedom Trail, visit Paul Revere's pathway, check out the Boston Tea Party site, and all the other places from the American Revolution that was imprinted on my mind like a map in the eighth grade. I was also excited because I was actually playing "hooky" from doing any work for two days.

John declared that a visit to Faneuil Hall was a must. Indeed it was. Right here, in this very room, the seeds of discontent were birthed. The Colonists were sick of taxes on stamps, sugar, tea—you name it. Their attitude was "Enough was enough." Right here in this hall more than 200 years ago, the Colonists began plotting their emancipation from England.

Earlier that day, we had visited the JFK Library. Our hearts were a tad heavy as we exited the Library, both of us remembering what we were doing that fateful November day when the announcement of Kennedy's death stunned the world. Then we headed toward downtown, seeking a waterside eatery offering Boston's best in fantastic seafood. With grand luck, we found a restaurant called Jimmy's and settled in for a two-hour lunch to discuss what we had just viewed and experienced.

Back to our experience in Boston's Faneuil Hall. We were awed when we dropped into a concert by the Chopin Choir from Buffalo, New York. The choir performed the Litany of Our Lady of Ostrobrama, one of the celebrations during Boston's recognition of Polish Heritage Month. The majority of the program was not in English, but we didn't mind. Their voices were magical; the music spoke clearly to all that were there.

The choir's very last number, though, was performed in English . . . a song most Americans grew up with and one that sends chills up and down my back. The Chopin Choir of Buffalo inspired everyone with their rendition of the *Battle Hymn of the Republic*. Beginning with "Mine eyes have seen the glory of the coming of the Lord . . ." to "His truth is marching on," we were spellbound.

I couldn't get the words or the melody out of my head for weeks. As I walked down the street and on walkways to planes, I hummed it as I went along. Just thinking of the tune, the words, and phrasing made me stop and ponder.

The Hand of Spirituality

The *Battle Hymn of the Republic* was written during the Civil War. The men and women of the time were endowed with tremendous courage and faith. And that *faith, hope,* and their *beliefs* were encompassed in *spirituality*—primary factors of which they were. Your own faith, hope, beliefs, and spirituality are no different today. Without these, you don't allow yourself to deal with a full deck in the hand of life. One other ingredient I would add to your spirituality deck is *love.*

The second step in building confidence from Chapter Two is to delete negativity; to surround yourself with positive people and work within a positive environment. In my book, *When God Says NO,* I wrote that Yeses—wonderful Yeses— are waiting to come into your life, if you only invite them in. Yeses are out there in the midst of chaos, pain, tragedy . . . and "Noes."

Stories of Spirituality

In 1974, I presented my first public speech. At that time, I was a stockbroker with EF Hutton. Forty-five eager women virtually hung on my words and advice about investing. That speech led to workshops just for women on money management and to several books on the topic. I have spoken to hundreds of thousands of women and men and girls and boys since that first presentation.

Because of the wide range of topics that I research, write about, and speak on, I have the wonderful opportunity of listening to others' stories . . . stories of incredible journeys and adventures. Some are tremendously exciting; others are terrifying and traumatic. Many can be called soul searching and life changing.

The most common link in the thousands of personal

stories about overcoming adversity was that of *spirituality*—
its necessity in their lives. In some cases, it saved their
lives. Spirituality is a belief that something, someone, a
greater being, is out there with a blueprint for steering your
life. For me, this greater being is my belief in God.

What role does spirituality play in your life? When it
plays a significant part, you, too, will know you're not
alone in your challenges.

Houston, We Have A Problem

In 1995, the movie *Apollo 13* was released. I purchased the
video when it was offered in the stores. Why? Because the
movie's fabric is woven with the threads of *faith, hope,
belief, love* and, yes, *God*. Although I remembered the actual space flight of years past, I still gripped my seat as I
watched the video. I felt my heart pound from all the sus-
pense, and I ooohed and awed at the photography of the
spacecraft's travels between the moon and earth. I knew
the astronauts would make it back . . . but, still, I felt I was
riding with them, living through their every moment until
they were back on earth with their family and friends.

Throughout the movie, the presence of *love* was evident—the love between husband and wife, between parent and child, and among co-workers. They were all in it
together, for better or worse. When there is no *love*, it's
difficult to create caring, kindness, or any type of opti-
mistic beliefs in oneself and others.

Think about the love you have in your life. How can
you tap into its power to better support you in creating
caring and kindness toward yourself and others?

Throughout the movie, the presence of *hope* is inter-
twined from beginning to end. The hope of going on another mission, the hope of not getting a common childhood
disease—measles, the hope of solving life-threatening prob-

lems within the spacecraft and at Mission Control, the hope of returning to earth alive. If there had been no *hope*, why bother to try resolving any of the problems that presented themselves hour by hour?

Often, hope comes from a deep belief in your faith, and it keeps you going when the going gets tough. Don't give up. Give hope a try.

Throughout the movie, the presence of *belief* was demonstrated—belief and determination that the problems would be solved in time to save the three astronauts; belief that they would be strong enough to endure the immense physical and mental pressures that resulted from adversities of the voyage; belief that they would figure out a way to survive the extreme cold of outer space; belief that could filter and extend the air supply to stay alive in the lunar module on the journey back to earth. If there hadn't been a strong *belief* that the multitude of problems would be resolved, everyone would have thrown in the towel when they saw the command module turn into a deathtrap.

What do you believe in that could be strong enough to endure your greatest challenges and see you through your darkest nights? Turn off those voices that tell you to give up and begin believing in your own talents. Then others will believe in you, too, as the whole world believed in the astronauts.

Throughout the movie, the presence of *faith* was highlighted. Faith in self and in others—to build the needed problem-solving team while the astronauts were thousands of miles away from home base. They radioed "Houston, we have a problem . . ." None were "macho," each one knew their limitations—all the players knew they could not go it alone, they had to work together . . . period. Faith poured from the hearts of parents, spouses, children, friends, coworkers, clergy, the media . . . concerned people from all corners of the world. Even the news commentator great Walter Cronkite expressed hope, belief, and *faith* as he encouraged all of us to offer our prayers for their safe return.

Where does your faith come from? How can you develop a deeper sense of faith for yourself? Many turn to prayer and meditation, or join churches and synagogues where all gain a greater understanding by learning together.

Faith, hope, love, and belief anchor your spiritual foundation. If any ingredient is splintered or shattered, your spirituality is challenged. When my partner embezzled hundreds of thousands of dollars, when I found myself in surgery fighting for my life, when my two sons died—one an infant, the other 19—each time I found my sense of spirituality move onto the back burner of my life. And then, like a boomerang, it came back. It reminded me that I couldn't go it alone, that I had another partner. My spirituality, through my belief in God, would be there as a guide. An awesome experience.

Of course, the crew of Apollo 13 did make it back to Earth. The astronauts' families, friends, NASA, the President of the United States, Congress, the media, the world . . . everyone cheered. They learned they were not alone. I absolutely believe they would not have achieved their goal without love, hope, belief, and faith. Developing your own spirituality is a must to living a full life . . . one that you deeply feel is worth living.

JB's Keeper #24
**The combined spirituality of humanity
is indeed awesome.**

Chapter Twenty-Three

Attitude—It Will Break, or Make You

Most projects, whether at work or at home, can be broken down into smaller more workable stages. That big project won't seem like an insurmountable mountain that you can't find the time to tackle if you take the time to identify these stages. Some stages must follow another sequentially; others can be pulled out of turn. And some don't have to be finished at one sitting. There may be one stage that is easier for you than another—if it makes sense, do it first. By breaking a project into stages before you begin, you write the recipe for its successful completion.

Some of my of big projects involve creating books. The books I write have multiple stages to them. One of the stages is research—gathering usable material from piles of literature and/or conducting a study or survey of the general public. The next stage is the analysis of the research.

It is one that identifies material to support the themes and key points used throughout the book.

If a survey is elemental in a book, the next stage is follow-up interviews. These interviews are the basis for the stories of the not so famous you find in my books. They probe into the reasons behind their responses on the questionnaires they completed. The interviews are often taped (though some are done in my infamous indecipherable handwriting), so the next stage is to transcribe/translate them. Another stage is determining where, or if, the individual interview will fit into the book.

Putting the Puzzle Together

I now have a lot of pieces that are not unlike the pieces of a giant puzzle you might dump on the table. They make no sense until you put like pieces in different piles as you would to solve a picture puzzle. At this stage, I outline the book and decide what pieces go where—what follows what.

Finally, there's the actual writing. This stage is one that cannot, of course, be done in a single sitting and so is divided into many sub-stages. When I sit down to write, I often focus on a part or parts that I feel energized by and enthusiastic about. Sometimes, though, I have to bite the bullet and struggle through a chapter that is complex.

When you read a book, you may read it from the preface and/or introduction straight through to the end. Or, you may select a chapter that speaks to a need you have. An author usually takes the latter route; few write from page one to page 300 in that exact order. The writing gets done in bits and pieces, and, as the words flow, bridges form between the chapters. It is not an overnight project and takes many months—sometimes, years. But it's the attitude the writer takes during each stage that brings the puzzle together to produce a successful book.

Removing the Sabotage Trap

Self-sabotage can be likened to erecting a barbed wire fence around yourself. Your ability to move on to other enterprises or personal pursuits is substantially inhibited— you have difficulty getting out and others rarely want to get scratched by trying to get in. You have isolated and insulated yourself from the truth of your situation. If you truly want to say, "Don't fence me in" to a self-sabotage trap, you first have to be aware of how and when you work against yourself.

When Kristi Yamaguchi won the gold medal at the Winter Olympics, commentator and former gold Olympian Scott Hamilton, remarked, "Kristi's strength is her lack of weakness." Denial that you are self-saboteur— denial that you haven't built that fence with the barbs of negative self-talk, procrastination, or being too personal— is counter productive to being the champ you can be.

If you are not pleased with your life, acknowledge that there is a problem. By recognizing weaknesses and areas you have relegated to self-sabotage, you can initiate a concentrated effort to eliminate them from your life. Are you alone? Absolutely not--everyone has practiced the art of self-sabotage at some time or another. Ralph Waldo Emerson said, "You are what you think you are . . . all day long." What are your thoughts during the day?

Throughout the chapters in this book, I have encouraged you to get appropriate feedback. Everyone needs it, whether it's accolades or caring criticism (and that's not an oxymoron). You need to know how you are doing on a regular basis.

Take advantage of Employee Assistant Programs. The EAP's primary purpose is to help employees overcome problems that interfere with their productivity. It could involve drugs, smoking, gambling, money, abuse, and other types of self-sabotaging behavior. If your company uses an EAP (ask in Human Resources), you have a big advantage.

First of all, EAPs work regularly with individuals whose negativity (self-sabotage) and problems are impacting their performance. Second, the company pays for this service so you don't have to. Seek other resources that include psychologists and career counselors. Get references and interview them before you begin work with either of these groups. The bottom line is that, if you have a problem, you don't have to tough it out alone. Get help!

Whenever I do a keynote speech on *The Confidence Factor—Cosmic Gooses Lay Golden Eggs*, I always highlight the step, *Delete Negativity*. Though many regard positive thinking as lot of hooey, I don't. Is the glass half-empty, or is it half full? It depends upon how you look at it—your attitude.

I'm also not shy in saying that you need to remove—delete—the energy suckers in your life. Shelve the people who are negative—those who see the glass as half empty with no possibility of it being full at any time. Who needs people who have nothing good to say about anyone or anything at any time—the ones who walk through the door and open the conversation with a litany of the horrors in their lives?

Make Your Day

Norman Vincent Peale, the father of positive thinking, died in 1994. His book, *The Power of Positive Thinking*, has sold more than 20 million copies. His vision was timeless and his success phenomenal. After all, how many people do you know who are successful or have overcome adversities use "The Power of Negative Thinking" as their philosophy? There are times when optimists are right, and there are times when pessimists are right. The difference is that the optimist does something about the problem and the pessimist only whines about it. You get to choose which one you'll be.

Which of the following would the optimist likely do and which would the pessimist do?

1. Write down three things that you'd like to accomplish today—make a "TaDah" list. Examples could be picking up the laundry, going grocery shopping, completing a phone survey, reading, and writing a report. Then set a reward for completion of the list. When completed, you get a TaDah!

2. Identify three ways in which you could sabotage your successful completion of the items in #1. Examples: I'm too busy to do them all; I won't get credit for my report because my boss always takes credit for my work; I'd rather hear all the juicy gossip than focus on the phone survey; I'd rather go have a drink with the guys after work because my job stinks; the laundry will still be there tomorrow.

3. Identify three ways you can make people at work miserable enough to wish that *you* had stayed home and played "hooky." Example: don't listen and/or interrupt when they are talking; claim someone's work is your own; complain that your workplace is a rotten place to go every day; refuse to help out when everyone else is overloaded.

4. Come up with three excuses that defend your behavior in #3. Examples: they never help me out; no one ever listens to me so why should I listen to them; you took credit for the work I did last month; if you were more organized, you would get your work done.

5. Now, name five things that you could do for yourself and for others that would help you have a sabotage-

free day. Examples: Delegate something you don't have time for and offer to cover for that co-worker so that he or she can go see the kids' school play; tell everyone that you'd like their feedback on problem you all have so you can, in unison, confront the issue with management; be cheerful when you answer *any* phone, your attitude could be infectious and land your company a new contract; have some solutions ready for your boss when you are called on carpet for a failure (no whiney excuses today, thanks); take an article to work that keys in on a new bit of technology that could streamline something you and your co-workers hate to do; whip up their enthusiasm for change.

If you concentrated on premises 2, 3 and 4, you have guaranteed a miserable day for you and your co-workers. If you concentrated on the first premise, you are showing some optimism in your own life but you aren't sharing the wealth. If you concentrated on the fifth premise, your work environment would be a better place to be.

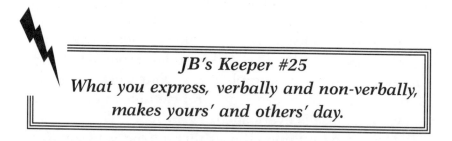

JB's Keeper #25
What you express, verbally and non-verbally, makes yours' and others' day.

Take the same attitude into your home and play, and you've achieved balance. Your efforts to improve your mental and physical surroundings will reduce your inclination to self-sabotage yourself. Crowd out negative elements with positive ones.

Your Attitude Makes the Difference

The phrase I remember best from the presidential election in 1992 came from the Democrats' camp — "It's the economy, stupid!" Those words shouted from a banner in Democratic Campaign Manager James Carville's office. The media found a real prize here. Everywhere I turned, that phrase popped up.

The reason these words received such notoriety was, I believe, because of the complicated scenarios the presidential candidates presented. Few really understood or cared to listen long enough to grasp them. But everyone knew that the economy, in particular deficit spending, was the prime concern of the citizenry. So the banner probably meant, "let's get down to basics—let's simplify."

To say or even intimate that you are or someone else is stupid can be called sabotaging behavior. But haven't you berated yourself about doing something stupid? The word "stupid" sends a clear message about your attitude. So let's concentrate on one simple concept—attitude. Self-sabotaging behavior can be non-existent if your attitude about yourself, your present position in life, and your future, are positive.

You might feel like saying, "It's not that simple, stupid." I would counter, "It's the attitude, stupid!" Actually, a friendlier motto could be:

"Attitude is Everything!"
Don't brag about what you can do . . . show the world what and that you can.

Your attitude can make or break you. While you work to combat the 21 ways to self-sabotage yourself as identified in this book, your attitude is the key to success in realizing your full potential in all areas of your life—today and tomorrow. "Poor me," "If it weren't for ___, I would," " I can't," are all attitudes self-saboteurs indulge in daily. They are as addictive as the most powerful drug known. But they are habits that can be broken.

Breaking out of old practices and habits isn't easy. But, with care and feeding, your attitude about yourself can improve. You will be able, in time, to look back at your old self and say, "I don't know that person, and I'm glad I don't."

> *Each day, you get to choose what face you put on—a pleasant one or a pissy one. Each day, you get to choose your humor and play quotients—abundancy or scarcity. Each day, you get to choose your interactions with you family, co-workers and friends—be present or distant. And, each day, you get to choose how you impact others—reach out in support or withhold it.*

The choice is yours. What will it be?

Chapter Twenty-Four

A Final Thought

No one is perfect. There will be times that you do yourself in. Sometimes just a bit; at others, major destruction. Most likely, you haven't set out to purposely undercut yourself. Yet at times, you have.

I truly believe that when you are willing to look yourself in the mirror, identify both strong and weak areas of how you function, you're then ready to make changes and move on.

Changes aren't easy. But, is anything that you really want easy or simple? Oscar Wilde said, "Experience is a name that everyone gives to their mistakes." You are going to make mistakes—they happen. And they do generate tons of experience. Ideally, your mistake/failure quotient will decrease as you eliminate the ways that you have undermined yourself in the past.

Eleanor Roosevelt said, "Do what you feel in your heart to be right—for you will be criticized anyway. You'll be damned if you do, and damned if you don't."

In the end, when you delete self-sabotage from your routine, you will find that you are far more productive, far more content, and far more passionate in both your personal and workplace lives. It's a win-win.

> *When you chose to recognize that inner snares exist and solutions could be found, that was good news. You now can deal with and learn how to zap self-sabotaging issues, behaviors, and methods.*
> *You've discovered that you can zap whatever enemies are at your gates including yourself.*
> *That's the great news!*

Acknowledgements

Books take time. That's the simple truth. *Stop Stabbing Yourself in the Back* took six years from the original idea to the publisher. It was heartening to hear audiences ask, "When will this book be here?—I need it now."

Ronnie Moore and WESType once again did her thing. I am always amazed what talents she brings to the publishing forum. Mikell Yamada again grasped my vision for the cover. I thank them both.

Shari Peterson and John Maling sharpened pencils and eyes—always responding to my query—does this make sense and does it flow?

Stop Stabbing Yourself in the Back—Zapping the Enemy Within contains thousands of voices of women and men today in and out of the workplace. I thank them for their time and sharing.

About the Author
Judith Briles, PhD, MBA

Dr. Judith Briles is CEO of The Briles Group, Inc. a Colorado based research, training and consulting firm. She is internationally acclaimed as a keynote speaker and recognized as an expert in solutions to workplace issues.

She is an award winning author of over 20 books including *Woman to Woman 2000, Changing Conflict to Collaboration, 10 Smart Money Moves for Women, Smart Money Moves for Kids, The Dollars and Sense of Divorce, Gender Traps, When God Says NO* and *The Confidence Factor.*

Dr. Briles has been featured on over 1000 radio and television programs nationwide and writes columns for the *Denver Business Journal, Colorado Woman News, MsMoney.com* and *iSPIRITUS.com.* Her work has been featured in T*he Wall Street Journal, Time, People, USA Today* and the *New York Times.* She's a frequent guest on *MSNBC, CNNfn and CNN.*

She is a director of the WISH List, serves on the Advisory Boards of Colorado Woman News, Zenith magazine and is a past director of the National Speakers Association, the Woman's Bank of San Francisco and Colorado Women's Leadership Coalition.

For information about Judith Briles' availability for speeches and subscribing to her newsletter, contact her at:

Judith@Briles.com or **DrJBriles@aol.com**
www.Briles.com

303-627-9179 ~ 303-627-9184 Fax
The Briles Group, Inc.
PO BOX 460880
Aurora, CO 80046